Praise for Sports Engineering

"At Pure Fishing, I am responsible for creating new spinning and spin cast fishing reels...I definitely enjoy my work, because I can personally relate to the use of the products. The great thing about being an engineer in this industry is that after a prototype is created, I do my best to test it on a beautiful stretch of water."

John Chapman
Director of Spinning Reel Development
Pure Fishing

"At K2, I designed snowboard footprints, profiles, and constructions with an emphasis on women's boards. I also organized and led on-snow tests on Mt. Hood for prototype testing. Gretchen Bleiler, the winner of the Women's Superpipe in the 2003 X-Games and the Women's US Open Halfpipe Championships rides my board!"

Stacie Glass
Former Snowboard Design Engineer
K2 Snowboards

"In my position at the U.S. Olympic Committee, I get to work with some of the best athletes in the world, and get to experience many sports that I never knew existed until I took this job. Many times the designers are also the "test pilots," so we get to try out a new instrumented boxing bag, take a luge sled down a start ramp, or paddle our instrumented kayak. Like I said before, I never know what to expect next, but I wouldn't want it any other way."

Tom Westenburg
Principal Engineer
United States Olympic Committee

"By working hard at developing my skills as an engineer, and being willing to say five simple words, the whole world becomes your oyster. The words? 'Yeah, I can do that.' Those five words and the ability to back it up is what gets you challenging work, fine homes, and fun cars to drive."

Kyle Milliken
Director of Project Management
Kinetek-De Sheng

"If you want to work in the golf industry, you must play and appreciate the sport or else you cannot design good products. A bachelor's degree is the minimum education, but we are finding that master's degrees are more valuable, and even PhDs are becoming common. The most important skills an engineering student can develop are to know their subjects very well, be deep but not narrow, be creative, proactive, and a good person."

Bing-Ling Chao
Director of Advanced Technology
Taylormade-Adidas Golf Company

**National Society of
Professional Engineers®**

HIGH TECH HOT SHOTS

Careers in Sports Engineering

By Celeste Baine

High Tech Hot Shots:
Careers in Sports Engineering
By Celeste Baine

Published by:
The National Society of Professional Engineers
1420 King Street
Alexandria, VA 22314
Phone: 703-684-2800 Fax: 703-836-4875
www.nspe.org

Copyright © 2004, Celeste Baine
First Printing 2004
Printed in the United States of America by United Book Press, Inc.
Art Direction/Design by MediaWorks Design

ISBN 0915409232

Publishers Cataloging-in-Publication Data
Baine, Celeste
High Tech Hot Shots, Careers in Sports Engineering. First Edition./Celeste Baine
Includes bibliographical references and index.
ISBN 0915409232 (pbk.)
1. Engineering—Vocational guidance.
2. Career education—handbooks, manuals, etc.
3. Engineering—study and teaching.
4. Sports—vocational guidance
"HIGHER." I. Title. II. Baine, Celeste.

How to Order:
Single copies may be ordered from NSPE at www.nspe.org or by calling 800-417-0348 and referencing NSPE Product #2200. Quantity discounts are also available. For more information, please contact the Director of Marketing, NSPE, 1420 King Street, Alexandria, VA 22314, 703-684-2800.

Warning—Disclaimer

ACKNOWLEDGEMENTS

Countless people generously contributed their time and energy to help me complete this project. The compilation of this book would have taken years longer without the help and support of the Women in Engineering Programs and Advocates Network (WEPAN) and the Society of Women Engineers (SWE), who provided contacts and ideas when I was hitting my head against the wall. I am grateful to the members who gave me a running start.

Special thanks also go to Steen Strand, Freebord Manufacturing Inc.; Dan Speranza; Cindy Hutter; James Page; Tom Westenburg; Stacie Glass; Betsy F. Willis, Ph.D., Southern Methodist University; Professor Dennis K. Lieu, University of California at Berkeley; John W. Chapman, EIT, Pure Fishing; Mark McNamee, EIT; Jennifer Ocif; Jay F. Humphries; Rebecca A. Farabaugh; Donald Loeffler, Wilson Sporting Goods; Georgena Terry; and Jeff Bresee, P.E. Without the profiles of the people above, this book would not be what it is today. We will all learn something from their experiences.

Extra gratitude goes to my peer reviewers for all their time and suggestions that made this book so much better: Cathy Pieronek, John McPhee, Herbert Yoo, Tom Westenburg, John Lehman, Elaine Seat, and Jon Doan. Your ability to steer me in the right direction was invaluable!

I would also like to thank Soraiya Dalal, Lisa Norwood, Robert P. Townsend, Bing-Ling Chao, Laurent Hanen, Jong-on Hahm, Kyle Milliken, Dolores Schafer Thompson, Jennie Caudle, Dan Barch, Tony Keller, Michelle Sabick, Linda Batz, Lisa Ackerman, Jessica Fusaro, and Barbara Ruel for their generosity and good-will.

Thanks also to my mom and dad for making me a fighter and upstream swimmer. And a big thank-you goes to my family for sharing their time with this project.

Lastly, I want to thank Terry Ames, director of marketing, and the National Society of Professional Engineers for supporting this project, seeing the possibilities, and wanting to make engineering more appealing and fun.

TABLE OF CONTENTS

ABOUT THIS BOOK 1

CHAPTER 1—SPORTS ENGINEERING AND YOUR FUTURE 3
  Sports Engineering 101 3
  Creative Engineering 9

CHAPTER 2—THE SPORTS 13
  Skateboarding 13
  Bowling 18
  Golf 24
  Tennis 32
  Inline Skating 38
  Fishing 43
  Baseball and Football 48
  Snow Sports 54
  Bicycling 62
  Swimming 67
  Parathletes 73

CHAPTER 3—SPORTS SUPPORT CAREERS .79
  Helmets 79
  Shoes 85
  Broadcast Engineering 91
  Food for Athletes 96

CHAPTER 4—SPORTING FACILITIES 101
  Stadiums, Arenas, Tracks, and Courses 101

CHAPTER 5—GETTING STARTED 109

GLOSSARY 119

BIBLIOGRAPHY AND RECOMMENDED READING 123

INDEX 129

About This Book

Consider this book a gateway. It is designed to open your mind to the wonders of engineering. You will see, first hand, the hundreds of things that you can do with an engineering degree and an interest in sports. You will discover opportunities you hadn't thought about, and you may even begin to look at engineering in a new way. Be prepared to get excited and to learn that engineering can give you a new and different way of seeing the world.

Written for middle school, high school, and pre-engineering college students, this book compiles resources, information, and stories of engineers who work passionately in the sports industry to design new and improved products for athletes and spectators, alike. Ranging from the design and construction of stadiums and courses to the design and manufacture of skateboarding, golf, swimming, and skiing equipment, as well as shoe design and much more, you will understand what you need to know to work in this industry and find a satisfying and rewarding job as a sports engineer.

This book presents possibilities you never expected. You will see what types of engineers create your favorite sports equipment and find out how to identify companies that will hire you as an engineer. From the software engineers who design scoreboards to the materials engineers who work on new helmets to the mechanical engineers who create new "extreme sports" products, the sports industry has a place for almost every type of engineer. You will learn what it takes to design sporting goods and get advice from engineers about how to succeed as a sports engineer. A strong motivation for writing this book is to help you see that engineering can be fun. It's fun being on the cutting edge of technology, and it's exciting to try to make the world a better place in which to live in.

If you have ever played a team sport, you understand that teamwork is integral to the success of the team. Each player brings different strengths to the team, without which the team can't function as efficiently. Engineering design works in the same way. Each member of the team contributes, according to his or her individual strengths, and, as a result, the learning produces an excellent product.

A vital component of engineering success, especially in the sports engineering industry, is excellent communication skills. As explained by Jennifer Ocif, a performance footwear engineer at Reebok International

Ltd., "Communication is a life skill that constantly needs attention and improvement. Unfortunately, it is not specifically taught in engineering classes, but you can learn it by doing it anywhere. You just have to work at it, because, no matter how smart you are, if you can't communicate with the people you work with, your ideas will never go anywhere."

Because the sports industry is so large, I can't cover every sport in this book. Some sports may be left out entirely and some descriptions may leave you craving more information. If you find yourself in the craving-more-information category, use that energy to your benefit. Contact the manufacturers listed to inquire about summer work or co-op opportunities. Tour facilities and begin talking to engineers for tips on getting through school and for gathering information about what they do now. Take apart your favorite piece of equipment to figure out how it works. Then, you'll truly begin to think and work like a sports engineer. Don't be afraid to fail a few times, either.

Thomas Edison was one of the most prolific inventors of all time. What made Edison so great was that he believed that every failure brought him closer to success. As a result of a lifetime of work and tens of thousands of failures, he held over 1,000 patents for his successful inventions. Failure is a rite of passage to success.

Some of the most amazing inventions and technologies on the market today exist because one engineer had an idea. Look back at old pictures of the bicycle. People wanted it to go faster, they wanted it to go down mountains and wanted it to be more comfortable. The difference is engineering. Year after year, engineers returned to the drawing board and made the bicycle better. What will bicycles look like in another 10 years? It's up to you and your imagination to make the world a better place—a place that is safer, more fun, and enjoyable for everyone.

If you want an exciting and diverse career, an engineering degree can blow open the doors of opportunity.

So lace up your running shoes and let's get going....

For current links to all Web sites listed in this book, visit: www.hightechhotshots.com and use the following username and password for access: Username: nspe
Password: sports

Chapter 1

Sports Engineering and Your Future

SPORTS ENGINEERING 101— I WANT TO RUN FASTER, JUMP HIGHER, AND HIT HARDER

The sports industry provides entertainment, physical fitness, and health awareness for millions of people around the world. This field is wide open and growing so rapidly that opportunities are plentiful and imaginative. Sports engineering is an excellent way to have an impact on athletes, sports, and businesses around the world, and sports engineers are some of the most dynamic, innovative, and creative engineers on the planet. This profession is full of diversity, fun, and intriguing opportunities, and most of the engineers working in the sporting goods industry became engineers because they love sports and want to improve either their own performance or the sport overall. A company that wants to design a new golf club for Tiger Woods would prefer to hire an engineer who has some experience with golf. A company that is designing new high-performance mountain bikes would prefer to hire an engineer who has a keen interest in bike design or racing bicycles. The industry offers some awesome careers for athletically inclined engineers!

Sports engineering is the bridge between classical engineering and sports science. Sports engineers use technology to analyze the equipment, the materials, and the mechanics of sports, athletes, and movement. These engineers strive to prevent injuries and to increase the achievement of athletes around the world. As a sports engineer, you can work to improve performance for all athletes, increase the fun and recreation of dedicated fans, and raise the image of all engineers.

Recreational sports date back at least 4,500 years, to a ski found in Hoting, Sweden. But, only recently, has the sports engineering industry boomed, as athletes have sought improved equipment and technology to better their performance. Sports engineering helps to break down each sport into its most basic elements (stride length, foot placement, swing speed, etc.) so that engineers can make tiny adjustments that result in bigger improvements in performance.

Classical Engineering

Engineering offers a progressive, challenging, and rewarding career. Individuals who have earned their bachelor's degree in engineering enjoy some of the highest paychecks of all baccalaureate graduates and have almost limitless career opportunities. Engineering is the second largest profession in the nation; there are almost 2.2 million engineers in the workforce. To succeed as an engineer in the competitive and challenging sports engineering industry, you must be willing to make the effort to excel in school and not let anything stand in your way. You have to know what you are getting into and have a clear idea about what you want.

The role of the engineer is perhaps one of the least understood in society. We see doctors, lawyers, and police officers on television, but where are the engineers? What do they do? Engineers use math and science in practical ways to benefit mankind. People have always held engineers in high regard; after all, engineers make the world go around. Most technological advances—automobiles, computers, the Internet, medical devices, the space shuttle, airplanes, robots, renewable energy—can be attributed to the work of engineers.

A degree in engineering opens many doors. Individuals who become engineers want to improve society; reduce pollution; end world hunger; invent exciting, cutting-edge technology; make life more convenient; or develop new theories to change the ways we think about the world. Anyone who is up to the challenge and has a genuine interest in taking things apart, solving puzzles and problems, or understanding nature can succeed.

Sports Science

In sports science, students learn the science of how the body works through biomechanics, human anatomy, human physiology, movement anatomy, and exercise physiology. To succeed in sports science requires paying close attention in science class and understanding biology, chemistry, and physics. Other courses include psychology, sociology, coaching, education, motor skill acquisition, nutrition, resistance training, exercise programming, sports injury, and exercise rehabilitation.

Before every Olympic summer game, the scientific community from around the world gathers to exchange ideas, developments, and findings in the Pre-Olympic Congress. The Congress is designed to bring all sports fields together to share research and developments in the field. It is one of the largest gatherings of cutting-edge research and performance improvements in the sports industry.

Sports Engineering

Engineers in the sports industry must have a solid and well-rounded knowledge of materials, equipment, and technology and familiarity of sports and athletics. Interpersonal skills are also a must, because the sporting goods industry is a people-oriented business. You must be able to work with athletes and others to ensure that your products meet the needs and requirements of the sport.

Many people don't realize how engineering plays such a big part in the sporting goods world. Millions of dollars are spent each year on research and development for new equipment and technology. Thousands of professional engineers contributed to the previous Olympic games and many more contribute daily to make professional sports more enjoyable and fun. For example, civil engineers spent two years building the bobsled, skeleton, and luge tracks for the 2002 Olympic games in Salt Lake City. A mechanical engineer developed the machine to make the snow that appeared on the ski jumps at the

Utah Olympic Park. Electrical engineers designed the state-of-the-art timing systems to ensure accuracy to 1/1000 of a second. Other engineers designed the bicycle track for the 1996 Olympics in Atlanta and many more worked on devices or technology to make all the other events in those 17 days of fierce competition more exciting and dramatic. This field is driven by innovation and the creativity that comes from applying knowledge already achieved into new situations to find new solutions.

How High Can You Jump?

Suppose for a moment that you are a high school student on the varsity basketball team. You're not sure if you have the skill to play professionally but enjoy the sport of basketball more than anything else in

your life. By studying engineering as an undergraduate college student, you can not only continue to play the sport but also develop the problem-solving capabilities that contribute to the sport in many ways. For example, as a materials engineering student, you may find new materials for court floors or shoes that can lessen knee and ankle injuries. As a mechanical engineer you may work hard to find new materials for bats that will enable a batter to hit the ball much farther and reduce the unwanted "sting" of the bat associated with hitting the ball off-center.

Engineers who work hand-in-hand with professional athletes have the perfect complementary relationship. Athletes hold the skills for their sports, while engineers complement that skill with their knowledge of technology and problem solving. Only when these two forces come together can you achieve the results that bring fans to their feet to cheer wildly and enthusiastically for the athlete. While the athlete is the star, the sport wouldn't be the same without the work of engineers behind the scenes.

Sports engineering does not fit within only one type or branch of engineering. Almost any type of engineer can find a role to play in sports engineering. The most common degrees of engineers within the field are mechanical, civil, materials, electrical, chemical, biomedical, industrial, and manufacturing engineering. The degree chosen should be based on personal preferences and interest.

Better training techniques, nutrition, and coaching have helped to improve the performance of athletes. Improvements in training and physiology, in conjunction with technological advancements, help to take the athletes further much faster. Very often, the introduction of new technology to aid in the sport can increase the performance in an unexpected way. For example, pole-vaulters have increased their vaults from just over 117 inches in the late 1800s to 241.75 inches in a 1994 competition. In 1964, glass fiber composite poles, although expected to give the jumper a higher jump, worked to help jumpers change their style to go over the bar feet first and, thereby, increase the vaulted height. Other engineers were needed to support the increased vaults by designing improved landing areas.

Another important aspect of sports engineering concerns how the evolution of new technology helps to prevent injuries. The advances of technology that make sports more enjoyable and more dynamic are wonderful for athletes and spectators but sometimes come at an unex-

pected cost. In the 1950s, football players were at high risk of head injuries because they didn't wear helmets. The engineers who designed the plastic helmets never imagined that they would create a much more dangerous sport, but the players perceived that they were safer because of the helmets and, therefore, took more risks. As explained by J.N.

Gelberg, author of *The Lethal Weapon: How the Plastic Helmet Transformed the Game of Football*, "Now that players can also tackle each other below the waist, football neck injuries have more than tripled and cervical spine injuries have doubled." The engineering design must always evolve to keep up with the changes in the sport and attitudes of the participants.

Innovative Thinking

Nike has established a new solution to the old problem of throwing away worn-out shoes. Now we don't recycle just cans, bottles, and paper. Through Nike's Reuse-A-Shoe program, the company takes used athletic shoes of any brand and grinds them to make cushioned playing surfaces. Approximately 2,000,000 pairs of shoes each year are ground. According to Nike, "We have three distinct types of Nike grind material: rubber from the outsole, foam from the midsole, and fabric from the shoe's upper. With the help of our licensee partners, we take the granulated rubber that comes from the shoe outsole and factory scrap and make soccer, football, and baseball fields and weight room flooring. We use the granulated foam from the shoe midsoles for synthetic basketball courts, tennis courts, and playground surfacing tiles. The granulated fabric from the shoe uppers becomes the padding under hardwood basketball floors. Not bad for a pair of old, worn-out shoes." Through the Reuse-A-Shoe program, Nike has contributed to the donation of more than 150 high-performance sport surfaces to communities around the world where kids wouldn't otherwise have access. Nike engineers have taken the knowledge gained from their own product development and applied it in an innovative way to help the environment and our schools. The surfaces also reduce athletic injuries caused by running on hard and inflexible surfaces.

CREATIVE ENGINEERING— WHAT IT TAKES TO SUCCEED

"By working hard at developing my skills as an engineer, and being willing to say five simple words, the whole world becomes your oyster. The words? 'Yeah, I can do that.' Those five words and the ability to back it up is what gets you challenging work, fine homes, and fun cars to drive."

Kyle Milliken
Director of Project Management
Kinetek-De Sheng

Sports engineering is not an accredited degree at any university in the U.S. and there is no one degree that is best suited to becoming a sports equipment designer. However, a genuine desire to succeed and a healthy appreciation for sports can get you in the door at most equipment companies.

Kyle Milliken, a mechanical engineer for an international manufacturing facility in Huizhoua, China, said, "To me, engineering is not a job but a way of seeing things and can lead to literally a world of opportunities. This 'way of seeing things' or perspective is the key and essential ingredient to being an engineer. Walt Disney wants a new thriller ride to delightfully terrify visitors at the park—some person grabs a piece of paper and starts sketching. A million pounds of aluminum, jet fuel, people, and food goes rumbling down the runway and takes flight—it's because some person had an idea. A doctor inserts a tiny device into the beating heart of a patient and their life becomes better—it's because somebody had a concept. Engineers are those people. Engineers turn ideas into reality. The vision, the ideas, and the concepts are the important part; math is just a tool that engineers use to do it."

Sophie Woodruff, an undergraduate student in Sports Product Design at South Bank University in London, England, said, "In my brief two years as a design student, I have learnt that sports design does not just entail engineering principles, as is the case in most product or engineering design situations. To design a great sports product, the designer must understand why the product is of such great importance to the athlete and how to maximize the success of such products whilst knowing how they work in conjunction with the human body."

Engineering is a rigorous major. The pursuit of an engineering degree is likely to challenge, frustrate, and confound you. Similar to any sport, to become one of the best takes perseverance, self-discipline, enormous amounts of effort, concentration, and a keen focus on your goal. You have to know that your goal will be worth it in the end and that you are doing something that gives you a sense of satisfaction and happiness.

Creativity and innovation are the keys to bringing designs to the marketplace. To be a successful sports engineer you must under-

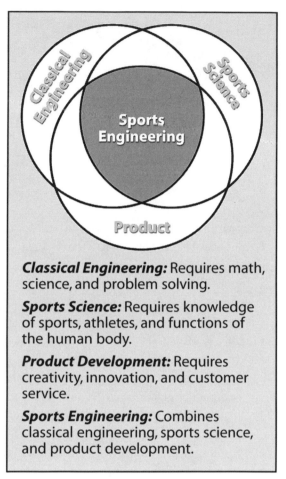

Classical Engineering: Requires math, science, and problem solving.

Sports Science: Requires knowledge of sports, athletes, and functions of the human body.

Product Development: Requires creativity, innovation, and customer service.

Sports Engineering: Combines classical engineering, sports science, and product development.

stand the sport, the performance criteria, and the perception of the fans. You must appreciate the mental state of both the athlete and the audience. Equipment must be designed to keep the athlete safe and to lessen injury. The social appeal of color, function, and trend must act as a unit. The materials should be the best for the conditions or developed to advance the sport. And lastly, the equipment must be thoroughly tested and evaluated. If problems are detected, you must work on redesign until your designs pass the important test and evaluation process.

Robert Townsend, a plastics engineer for DuPont Packaging and Industrial Polymers, said, "Although my degree is in engineering, all of my 20-year career has been in sales or market development. I enjoy the people contact and working directly with customers. My engineering background allows me to converse with and understand their needs." According to Townsend, "To be a good sports engineer, you must conduct market research and personal interviews to gain 'the voice of the customer.' You must gain a better understanding of what their problems are, what their vision is, and where they want to be in the future. Sports equipment design is a competitive environment, and you need to understand what solutions exist to help the customer get what they want. The skills that are helpful include: paying attention to detail, being diligent and persistent, staying to committed schedules, staying abreast of industry/market trends."

Laurant Hanen, a materials engineer for DuPont France, said, "We at DuPont don't pretend to know how to make a bicycle, a roller, or a ski binding. But we know which resin to use, how to design and mold a plastic part. This is where sport brands need our support. We are experts in finding the good match between a polymer and an application."

Chapter 2

The Sports

SKATEBOARDING

Steen Strand, Mechanical Engineer
and Founder of Freebord Manufacturing Inc.

Steen Strand studied economics at Harvard and started his career as an investment banker on Wall Street. After three years, he felt that working only with numbers was too much of an abstraction and that he needed to work with real, tangible objects. He eventually enrolled in the product design program at Stanford University where his passion for snowboarding led him to create a street-based snowboard simulator as part of his master's degree thesis in mechanical engineering. "I wanted to duplicate the snowboard ride," said Strand, "and that meant creating something that would slide as well as carve." Conventional skateboards can mimic carving, but not sliding or spinning. Strand engineered more than 40 prototypes or models to develop his concept. After graduation, he founded Freebord Manufacturing to produce the boards. His customers include diehard snowboarders who are desperate to ride even when there is no snow. "Snowboarders are like addicts—they go through withdrawal if they aren't riding. Freebord gets them through the summer and fills the months when they are too poor to buy lift tickets," said Strand.

Strand received two U.S. patents for the Freebord design, which

looks like a long skateboard with extra-wide trucks and two additional wheels. The extra wheels swivel 360 degrees and are adjusted closer to the ground than the outer four wheels. They also have a built-in spring bias that gently pushes them back into a straight position while the rider is maneuvering. "It stimulates the natural tendency of a snowboard to go straight" Strand said. "If you didn't have the spring bias, the wheels would act squirrelly, as if you were snowboarding on ice."

Because of the unique wheel configuration, the Freebord can rock from side to side, replicating the edge-to-edge sensation of a snowboard and enabling all of a snowboarder's maneuvers on pavement, including setting an edge to slow down. The Freebord also can be used just like a regular skateboard by adjusting the height of the center wheels relative to the outer wheels. Said Strand, "People give us the strangest looks because we'll throw huge drifting turns like we're in deep powder, then

set an edge and stop right in front of them. They think it's magic." Riding a Freebord down city streets in San Francisco on your first try will be a little tricky, but once you get it, you're hooked. Other than dodging the occasional car, the experience is almost identical to snowboarding.

Skateboarding Equipment Design Today

Skateboarding, the nation's sixth largest participant sport, was originally invented as a way to surf without water, or "street surf." There are 16 million skateboarders in the U.S. and more than 20 million worldwide. In the 1950s, frustrated surfers attached wheels to planks of wood and created the first skateboards. Today, skateboarding is extremely popular and can be seen as a symbol of adventurousness, individualism, and even rebellion. Skateboards and skateboard-related products from about 300 manufacturers of professional-level equipment generate $1.4 billion in annual retail sales. About 100,000 professional skateboard decks (boards) and 500,000 wheels are manufactured each month, leaving plenty of room for skateboard-loving engineers to find their perfect job. In California, alone, the International Association of Skateboard Companies estimates skateboarding employs more than 18,000 people. As

a further testament to the growing love of the skateboarding culture, the kids at Nickelodeon's Kids Choice Awards 2001 chose Tony Hawk, the world's most famous professional skateboarder, over basketball great Shaquille O'Neal as their favorite male athlete.

If you share the skateboarding passion, as an engineer you can design trucks, wheels, hardware, or skate parks. At first glance, it doesn't seem like very much engineering goes into skateboards, but, in fact, they are a creative blend of art and engineering. From the materials to make the board, to the wheels, to the trucks, skateboard engineers employ their engineering education to further a sport they love.

According to Tim Piumarta of Santa Cruz Skateboards, many boards use seven layers of sugar maple veneers. Engineers learned to use sugar maple because of its particular material properties, such as toughness and elasticity. The veneers are pressed together for 30 minutes to an hour in a press that can make three to five decks at the same time. The concave shape (curves up along the edges,

front, and back) of the board gives it strength and stiffness. After engineers design the proper curvatures, other engineers design the necessary molds using a CAD/CAM (Computer Aided Design/ Computer Aided Manufacturing) system to form the board into the required shape. After several days of curing, the final shape is cut out, and the board is machined and painted.

Ultimately, a well-designed skateboard makes the rider feel good. Does the rider have enough control? Will the rider be able to jump a flight of stairs without the skateboard breaking? Will the rider be able to "Ollie" the way the rider wants? According to Piumarta, "All the engineering in the world means nothing if it doesn't result in a good ride." For more information about engineering the skateboard, visit "Skateboard Science: The Art and Science of Skateboard Design" at the Exploratorium Museum in San Francisco: www.exploratorium.edu/skateboarding/skatedesign.html.

Engineers who do this include:

- **Civil Engineers**—May design skate parks that allow skaters to jump benches, slide down poles, maneuver over ledges and/or invent other obstacles that allow skaters to do tricks; design portable ramps and ledges for learning to do tricks at home or to allow skaters to set up a makeshift park anywhere they want; and work with city councils to get ordinances approved to build skate parks.
- **Electrical Engineers**—Design instrumentation to verify dynamic performance such as flex rates, landing spring, etc.; test and estimate break points for safety and reliability.
- **Manufacturing Engineers**—Determine systems to get the skateboard manufactured and are interested in reducing the costs associated with production, so more people can afford a better skateboard at lower prices.
- **Materials Engineers**—Always on the lookout for new materials to have more fun and provide a better ride. This includes

anything that makes up the skateboard (boards, wheels, trucks, grip tape, glues for pressing the boards, and everything else).

• **Mechanical Engineers**—May design the boards, trucks, wheels, bearings, and everything in between to improve the ride and function.

Skateboard-related companies that hire engineers:

The easiest way to find the company to work for is to go to www.skateboarddirectory.com. Click on "Skateboard Companies" and feast your eyes on all the opportunities that await you. A few of the more prominent manufacturers are:

• Alien Workshop—www.alienworkshop.com
• Birdhouse Skateboards—www.b-house.com
• Consolidated Skateboards—www.consolidatedskateboard.com
• District Skateboards—www.districtskateboards.com
• Eternal—www.eternalskate.com
• Girl Skateboard Company—www.girlskateboard.com
• Santa Cruz Skateboards—www.scskate.com
• Variflex—www.variflex.com
• Watson Laminates—www.watsonlaminates.com

More resources:

• California Amateur Skateboard League—www.caslusf.com
• International Association of Skateboard Companies—www.skateboardiasc.org
• Skatepark Association of USA—www.spausa.org
• Tony Hawk Foundation—www.tonyhawkfoundation.org
• United Skateboarding Association—www.unitedskate.com

BOWLING

Danny Speranza, Head of Research and Development, Columbia Industries

 At age eight, Danny Speranza was introduced to bowling, and he has made this sport his passion ever since. After graduating with a mechanical engineering degree from the University of Delaware, Speranza worked briefly for Allied Chemical before returning to his true love of bowling. As an engineer at AMF Bowling Corporation, Speranza worked on the first urethane bowling ball (the AMF Angle), patented a fiberglass lane, designed and patented the Spectrum ball return, and designed the HPL 9000 synthetic lane. From there, Speranza moved on to become the manager of the Equipment Specification Department at American Bowling Congress/Women's International Bowling Congress (ABC/WIBC) where he held that position for 10 years before arriving at Columbia 300 in 1996. Speranza's current duties at Columbia include directing, designing, and testing new ball releases. He also partners with BASF to develop new shell technology.

While at ABC/WIBC, Speranza designed and patented C.A.T.S.®, a Computer Aided Tracking System, for analyzing the path of the ball down the lane. Speranza worked with professors at the University of Wisconsin in Milwaukee to develop a mathematical model of the bowling ball path on the lane that includes factors such as varying friction, speed, rotation, ball Rg (radius of gyration, a measurement of the effective weight distribution in a ball as it relates to the moment of inertia; essentially, an indication of the resistance to rotation motion), and differential Rg (the difference between the minimum and maximum Rg axis in a ball, which determines the track flare potential; track flare increases the friction between the ball and the lane.) While at ABC/WIBC, Speranza developed the dynamic ball specifications for coefficient of restitution, coefficient of friction, Rg, and differential Rg and designed the test equipment to measure the properties. This technology has helped the game of bowling become more prominent and possibly an Olympic sport in the future.

An accomplished bowler himself, Speranza has 13 sanctioned 300 games and three sanctioned 800 series to his credit. He and Pam, his wife of 17 years, embraced the game so totally that they completed all the training to be Silver Level coaches through the ABC certification program. Only Silver Level coaches may apply to become Gold Level coaches, the best bowling coaches in the world. Speranza thoroughly enjoys sharing his vast knowledge and experience, both on and off the lanes.

Bowling Equipment Design Today

At first glance, bowling seems like an easy exercise for engineers. Engineers make a ball that weighs 14–16 lbs. and build a lane or path that the ball can roll on to knock down 10 pins at the end of the lane. The participants of the sport wear funny shoes and shirts and call themselves bowlers. You'd probably think that most of the engineering is in the pin resetter and ball return devices, right? Well, think again.

The engineering that goes into the sport of bowling is now so technologically advanced that an engineering degree is required to advance the sport. From bowling ball design to lane design to pin design, these engineers are at the top of their game. Don't be fooled into complacency by the seemingly casual recreation of the sport or the cosmic bowling alleys of late that play loud music, blow fog, and flash colored lights through the crowds.

The true art of bowling is to hit a one-inch-wide pocket that is 60 feet away. This tiny pocket is just off the center of the front pin and can be very elusive. When the ball hits the target, known also as a strike, the ball ricochets through the pins and knocks every one down. If you have ever watched bowlers in a bowling alley or on TV, you've probably said to yourself, "I can do that." Bowling looks easy.

Today, engineers have figured out how to create a ball that can smash into a larger two- to four-inch pocket to achieve the same result, because ball manufacturers have built a hook into the design. The standard pocket width for a ball rolling straight down the lane is only one inch. However, if you can hook the ball at an angle of at least six degrees when the ball enters the pocket, the size of the pocket jumps from one inch to two or three inches. Because of the precise engineering and understanding of the sport, this enlarged pocket has made the number of perfect games increase from 829 in 1964 to 44,363 in 2003. Additionally, according to the ABC, before 1999, no one had ever bowled three perfect games in a row. Between 2000 and 2003, five people achieved that feat. The designs of bowling balls have become so sophisticated that the balls practically seek the pins, and the outer coatings grip the lane like the tire of a dragster.

Bowling is one of those sports where every throw is unique. Every throw is unique because bowling alleys apply mineral oil on the lanes (most commonly made of pine, cherry wood, or a synthetic laminate) to condition them to take a continual pounding. The amount of oil on the lane, the type of oil, the lane material, the temperature, the humidity, and the type of bowling ball makes the outcome of every throw unpredictable. The amount of oil close to the pins is different from the amount of oil closer to the bowler. Likewise, the amount of oil on the outside of the lane is less than on the inside. No two bowling lanes have the same amount of oil; some alleys use different grades of oils, and some lane oiling machines disperse the oil differently on the lane. Could you guess that oil on the lane would make the bowling ball engineer's job so challenging? How would you design a bowling ball to roll down a lane that changed with every throw?

When a bowler releases the ball, that ball traveling down the lane, can reach a temperature of 1,400 degrees Fahrenheit (friction creates heat!) The ball pushes the oil around and creates an endless assortment of oil lines or tracks within the lane that, when followed by the next several bowling balls, can almost guarantee strikes for serious bowlers.

Bowling ball engineers also change the shape and density of the core of the ball so that it can gyrate (spin on its axis) and hook more or less. Some cores are shaped like bells, some have unusual patterns, and others may have spheres or ellipses. The composition of the inside of the ball can allow it to go slower or faster. The

outer surface or coating a designer puts on the ball can give it more grip on the lane or allow it to slide through the lane oil.

On a typical day, when a player throws a hook, the ball is released with

Examples of bowling ball cores.

a counter-clockwise rotation and first travels in a straight line as it slides through the oil. A few feet from the pins, when it exits the oil, the friction from the lane causes it to grip the lane and hook into the pins. It is the combination of all these variables that makes the job of the bowling ball engineer so fascinating and never routine.

Engineers, chemists, and ball testers spend hundreds of hours designing and evaluating different combinations of shells and cores for bowling balls. The perfect ball would grip better in oily conditions and hook better in non-oily conditions. Engineers use CAD software to design the core and shell of the ball to improve the performance. Most of the premanufacturing design that is created on the CAD system allows the designer to easily change the core shape and density in pursuit of the

> Soraiya Dalal, a chemical engineer with Columbia 300 got her job as a bowling ball engineer because she interned at Columbia during the summer before graduation from Trinity University. Dalal said, "Never, in a million years, did I ever think I would go into bowling design, but I love it! My job is unique, and I love talking to people about it, because they don't realize how much work goes into designing a bowling ball."

perfect strike-seeking design. Improvements in the core design change the physics of the ball and impact how it rotates. Early balls were made of hard polyurethane, and a bowler typically had one ball for all lanes and occasions. Today, balls are made of softer plastics and bowlers typically carry from four to eight to a tournament, to adjust for different amounts and grades of oil on the lanes, the temperature, and whether it is the first frame or second.

Bowling ball tests require the creation of a prototype or test model. According to Columbia 300, "After a prototype has been created, it is then ready for on-lane testing. The computer makes this job easier and allows the engineers to ensure that they are comparing apples to apples when comparing two balls. This is where the C.A.T.S.® (Computer Aided Tracking System) comes into play. Through a series of on-lane sensors, the computer tracks the ball speed and location at various points on the lane and calculates entry angle of the ball into the pins, all in the blink of an eye. The computer also puts this information into a database for comparison against other balls in the test group. The ball testers then add their notes regarding their observations for the ball. Even though the computer can give an engineer all the technical data, it is still feedback from the group of ball testers and sales that determines which prototypes become actual balls in the Columbia 300 line."

Engineers who do this:

- **Chemical and Materials Engineers**—May design balls, pins, synthetic lanes, ball polish, ball bags, and oil for lane conditioning.
- **Civil Engineers**—May design the bowling alley, itself.
- **Electrical Engineers**—May design new computerized scoring systems or cosmic bowling electrical systems.
- **Mechanical Engineers**—May design pin resetters, ball returns, lanes, scoring systems, ball testing systems, and bowling alleys.

Bowling-related companies that hire engineers:

- AMF Products—www.amf.com
- AZO Bowling—www.azobowling.com
- Brunswick Bowling and Billiards Corporation— www.brunswickbowling.com
- Clearballs.com—www.clearballs.com
- Columbia Industries—www.columbia300.com
- Ebonite—www.ebonite.com
- Lane#1—www.lane1bowling.com
- Morich Motion Tuned Core—www.morich.net
- Storm—www.stormbowling.com
- Track Bowling—www.trackbowling.com
- Visionary Bowling Products—www.visionarybowling.com

More resources:

- American Bowling Congress—www.bowl.com
- Billiards & Bowling Institute of America (BBIA)—www.billiardandbowling.org
- Bowl-Tech—www.bowltech.com
- Bowling Inc.—www.bowl.com
- Canadian Tenpin Federation—www.tenpin.org
- College Bowling USA (CBUSA)—www.bowl.com
- High School Bowling USA (HSBUSA)—www.highschoolbowlingusa.com
- International Association of Bowling Lane Specialists—www.nairbowl.org
- International Bowling Museum & Hall of Fame—www.bowlingmuseum.com
- Professional Bowlers Association (PBA)—www.pba.com
- Professional Women's Bowling Association (PWBA)—www.pwba.com
- The National Bowling Association (TNBA)—www.tnbainc.org
- Women's International Bowling Congress (WIBC)—www.bowl.com
- Young American Bowling Alliance (YABA)—www.bowl.com

GOLF

Rebecca Farabaugh,
Sporting Goods Segment Manager, DuPont Company

"At DuPont, I am responsible for developing and implementing market strategies and plans for the sporting goods segment. I also lead the cross-functional market segment team that is responsible for developing new products for this segment. I initially chose to study chemical engineering at the University of Delaware because I liked chemistry and math. In addition, I felt that a chemical engineering degree with a minor in business administration would provide me with a background that would offer the flexibility to ultimately work in the business and marketing area of a technology company.

"DuPont also offers a Field Engineering program that provides new engineers an opportunity to work in various areas of the company for two-year assignments. I felt this program would offer an excellent opportunity to obtain experience in various types of jobs very early in my career.

"I chose to work for DuPont because of the diverse technology-based products that they produce and the associated opportunities resulting from these diverse products. I really like the variety associated with my job. I get to work with our various business and technical groups in order to meet the needs of our customers. I also like the opportunity to directly interact with the customer as they work to design new products with our polymers.

"One of these products is the Surlyn® ionomer that is used for golf ball covers and the inner mantle layer. When Surlyn® was first introduced as a golf ball cover, it provided superior cut resistance versus other polymers that were available. But recently, DuPont introduced DuPont™ HPF polymer, the first in a series of new products that are specifically designed to be highly resilient and soft at the same time. This combination of properties allows the golf ball manufacturers to design golf balls for professionals and amateurs with improved distance, control, and feel."

Golf Equipment Design Today

Golf looks simple. On a beautiful day, you place the ball on a tee, swing at the ball with a carefully selected club, and try to get the ball to land in a little hole, usually anywhere from 150 to 400 yards away. If the ball doesn't go right into the hole, you walk to where the ball landed and hit it again until it rolls into the hole. The perfect green grass feels plush under your spiked shoes. The wind is minimal. How hard can it be?

Although golf may appear simple and the rules easy to understand, it takes a great deal of work to become the next Tiger Woods. Golf requires concentration, skill, luck, and the right equipment. Golf clubs are made to fit the golfer's body, course conditions, and weather. Golf balls need to match the course conditions, weather conditions, and the golfer's swing style and swing speed. There is much more to golf equipment design than meets the eye.

Golf Ball Design

Golf ball research and development has become a million-dollar industry. Over 850 million golf balls are produced each year, including balata balls; distance balls; spin balls; hard balls; soft balls; and one-, two-, and three- piece balls. There are balls for women, men, 0–10 handicappers, 11–20 handicappers, and more. Balls may be injection molded, with cores of different densities, elastic windings, multilayer covers, inner covers, outer covers, middle covers or Surlyn® covers. Golf ball design has become increasingly complex, and the engineers who design golf balls have backgrounds ranging from aerospace to mechanical to materials engineering.

There is no "right" ball for all golfers because the perfect ball for each person depends on how hard one hits it and how much spin one applies to each stroke. Designing the perfect golf ball requires an understanding of fluid dynamics and aerodynamics. Fluid dynamics affects how air passes over the ball. When a golf ball is hit, the air forms a boundary layer around the ball that reduces the drag. The dimples on a golf ball disturb the airflow around the ball and create turbulence. This turbulence increases kinetic energy, decreases drag, and creates a smaller wake, which improves the speed and distance of the ball's flight. Each ball usually has between 350 and 500 dimples, and the dimples can vary in depth and size. The dimples give the ball lift at slow speeds and reduce drag at high speeds. If the dimples are too shallow, the ball flies too high and not very far. If the dimples are too deep, the ball may go very far but won't allow the golfer to add any spin. Larger or deeper dimples can negatively affect the way the ball putts, especially at low speeds.

The main classes of golf balls are wound, solid, and multipiece cores. The balls can be composed of one, two, three, or four pieces. The outsides can be soft, medium, or hard. Engineers in this industry face many challenges to get the right golf ball to each golfer. A golfer with a fast swing needs a hard ball, although in very cold weather conditions, the golfer may prefer a medium hard ball. A golfer who depends on spin to make the ball roll a certain way when it hits the green will normally want to use a two- or three-piece ball; but if the grass is wet and prevents the ball from rolling, such a golfer may prefer a ball that doesn't depend on the spin applied.

To further challenge the engineer, the United States Golf Association (USGA) maintains strict golf ball manufacturing standards, so that no golfer has an equipment advantage over another. The USGA tests golf balls with a machine called "Iron Byron," which reproduces golf swings. The average professional golfer swings a driver at 109 mph, which produces a launch speed of 235 feet per second at a 10-degree angle. Iron Byron simulates a golfer's swing repeatedly, so the USGA can test new golf balls to ensure that they meet the standards specified. All of the following golf ball parameters include a 6% margin of error.

- Minimum Size (Diameter) = 1.680 inches
- Maximum Weight = 1.62 ounces
- Maximum Distance with Iron Byron = 296.8 yards
- Maximum USGA Initial Velocity = 255.0 feet per second

To engineer the longest-flying golf ball, an engineer must strive to design as close to USGA specifications as possible. The endless variables in design, increasing interest in the sport, and new lines of balls every year will ensure job security for the golf ball engineer.

Golf Club Design

A "Driver"

The golf clubs in a player's bag usually include drivers, woods, irons, wedges, and putters. The drivers and woods are the large bulbous-headed clubs that are made from wood, nickel, plastic, metal, and/or titanium. The shafts are made of graphite, boron, and stainless steel.

The drivers are designed to hit from the tee and make the golf ball travel as far as possible. Engineers also try to design the clubs so that any off-center hits produce the best results possible. The most frequently used clubs in the bag are the irons and wedges. They are the metal-looking numbered clubs that can hit the ball nearly as far as the driver, or they can make the ball fly very high over a short distance. Looking at just the driver provides some insight into the most desirable golf club.

To make the ball travel as far as possible, the golf club shaft must be stiff for

Golf clubs called "Irons"

Different putter designs

players with very fast swings or of medium stiffness for players with slower swings. A player who can swing like a professional needs a very stiff shaft so that the maximum amount of energy is transferred from the swing to the ball. A player who has a slower swing might desire some flexibility in

the shaft on the down swing to allow the club to "whip" and add extra energy to the ball at contact.

Increasing the moment of inertia is a trick that golf club designers can implement to make the ball go farther and the club more forgiving. Increasing the moment of inertia increases the size of the "sweet spot" (area) on the club face that delivers the best hit. If the ball is hit off-center and misses the "sweet spot," the club head typically rotates slightly from the impact and causes a slice or hook. This happens often to inexperienced golfers who hit their balls into the trees or off the fairway. Bigger club heads and new club face materials are both helping to make the "sweet spot" larger and more forgiving.

Another aspect of golf club design is the coefficient of restitution (COR). The COR is the amount of rebound that the materials of a club face give the ball or, more precisely, the energy conserved from a collision between two objects. COR is a measure of the impact between the ball and the club. For example, when the club hits the ball, the club face deflects slightly and then the material rebounds to give the ball extra kick. If the COR = 0.00, all energy is lost in the collision and the ball sticks to the club face (it does not bounce off). If the COR = 1.00, no energy is lost (no heat is produced, no sound is made, and no vibration occurs). A golfer swinging a club with a COR of 0.86 at 100 mph will hit the ball 5.6 yards farther than if he uses a club with a COR of 0.83. Engineers have designed drivers that are so efficient (high COR) that the USGA decided to put a limit on the COR. A maximum COR of 0.83 or higher is now considered illegal.

Bing-Ling Chao, director of advanced technology at Taylormade-Adidas Golf Co., explained, "If you want to work in the golf industry, you must play and appreciate the sport or else you cannot design good products. A bachelor's degree is the minimum education, but we are finding that master's degrees are more valuable, and even PhDs are becoming common. The most important skills an engineering student can develop are to know their subjects very well, bc deep but not narrow, be creative, proactive, and a good person."

Rebecca Farabough, an engineer at DuPont suggested, "Try to obtain a summer job or internship in an engineering-related job. This will provide you with valuable first-hand experience about what an engineer really does in the industry and will be very good experience to report on your resume and for discussion during interviews."

Engineers who do this:

- **Aerospace Engineers**—May design golf balls or systems to analyze the aerodynamics of new designs.
- **Electrical Engineers**—May design computer systems to analyze golf swings, computer software for course layout or water runoff, and design golf cart GPS systems.
- **Manufacturing Engineers**—May design golf ball or club manufacturing systems.
- **Materials Engineers**—May design golf ball materials, such as new covers or cores, or design new grips.
- **Mechanical Engineers**—May design new computer programs to analyze airflow around the ball, design golf carts, design golf ball or club manufacturing machines, find new ways to produce clubs, or design new clubs.

Golf-related companies that hire engineers:

- Accu-Flex Golf Shafts (golf club shafts)—www.accuflexgolf.com
- AccuPro Golf (custom clubs)—www.accuprogolf.com

- Arnold Palmer Golf (irons, woods, putters, and junior clubs)— www.arnoldpalmer.com
- Bell Golf (irons, woods, wedges, grips, and shafts)— www.bellgolf.com
- Callaway Golf (maker of the famous Big Bertha line of clubs)— www.callawaygolf.com
- Ceramic Advantage LLC (putters and woods)— www.ceramicgolf.com
- Dunlop Golf (clubs and accessories)—www.dunlopgolf.com
- Dynacraft (club components and club-making videos)— www.dynacraftgolf.com
- Fenwick Golf (shafts)—www.fenwickgolf.com
- Golf Pride Grips (grips)—www.golfpride.com
- GolfSmith (woods, putters, balls, and more)— www.golfsmith.com
- Grafalloy (ultra-lightweight shafts)—www.grafalloy.com
- Infiniti Golf (merged metal technology woods and putters)— www.infinitigolf.com
- Innovative Graphite (graphite shafts)—www.innographite.com
- Liquidmetal Golf (drivers, putters, bags, and more)— www.lmgsportsinc.com
- Louisville Golf (woods, putters, and drivers)— www.louisvillegolf.com
- MacGregor Tourney (irons, woods, putters, wedges, and bags)— www.macgregorgolf.com
- MasterGrip (clubs and accessories)—www.mastergrip.com
- Maxfli (clubs, balls, gloves, and accessories)—www.maxfli.com
- Nicklaus Golf (woods, irons, shafts, putters, and more)— www.nicklaus.com
- Orlimar (club line featuring TriMetal technology)— www.orlimar.com
- Ping (irons, woods, putters, and more)—www.pinggolf.com
- Raven Golf (woods, irons, shafts, and accessories)— www.ravengolfclubs.com
- Royal Precision (club shafts and grips)—www.royalprecision.com
- Scientific Golfers, Inc.—www.scientificgolfers.com
- Tacki-Mac Grips (do-it-yourself grip kits)—www.tackimac.com

- Taylor Made Golf (woods, irons, putters, and more)—www.taylormadegolf.com
- Titleist (golf equipment)—www.titleist.com
- Top-Flite (balls, drivers, irons, and more)—www.topflite.com
- Tour Edge Golf (irons, woods, putters, and shafts)—www.touredge.com
- True Temper Sports (steel and graphite shafts)—www.truetemper.com
- Wilson Sporting Goods Co. (clubs, balls, bags, and accessories)—www.wilsonsports.com
- Winn Grips (grips)—www.winngrips.com

More Resources:
- Club Design and Construction —www.swingweight.com
- Golf Information Directory—www.golflink.com
- Ladies Professional Golf Association—www.swingweight.com
- USGA—www.usga.org

TENNIS

Donald Loeffler, EIT,
Performance Racquet Design Engineer, Wilson Sporting Goods

"Growing up, I wanted to design roller coasters. It was my dream. As I began researching how to get there, I learned it would take a degree in engineering to fulfill this dream. My grandfather was an engineer, so I felt I already knew a little bit about what it would take to be an engineer.

"During my freshman year at Purdue University, a required class dealing with all the various disciplines of engineering introduced me to my major, mechanical engineering. Mechanical seemed to be the most

versatile form of engineering, and that really appealed to me.

"At Purdue, the top one-third of the class is offered the opportunity to be in a cooperative education (co-op) program. Following your freshman year, a student can enroll in the co-op program and alternate semesters between working at a company and going to school; basically, turning a four-year program into a five-year program, but you graduate with valuable work experience. Wilson Sporting Goods was my first choice, because tennis has always been one of my passions. I played competitively through high school and worked as an assistant tennis professional giving lessons at a local country club. My tennis experience and knowledge of racquets, along with my performance in the classroom at Purdue, helped me get the Wilson co-op position.

"As a co-op student, I was involved in the testing and analyzing of racquets and tennis balls. I measured the physical properties, such as length, weight, and inertia, to determine how a new design was going to perform. There is so much to learn in this industry that I was constantly fascinated by the dynamics of the design process.

"After receiving my degree from Purdue I began working full-time as a design engineer in January of 2003. Wilson employs three design engineers: the performance racquet engineer, an accessories engineer, and an indoor sports (racquetball/badminton/squash) engineer. On any given day, I often combine the knowledge I acquired at school with the skills I learned while working as a co-op, to arrive at the best answer or solution. Only 18 months after graduation, I am now Wilson's primary performance racquet engineer. Performance racquets are the racquets sold in sporting goods stores and pro shops without strings. These racquets are typically more expensive and used by serious recreational players or professionals. I give my input regarding the design from start to finish, watching the design process from prototype through production. Without my engineering degree and my years of playing tennis, I wouldn't be here today.

"It's been overwhelming at times, but I'm happy I've stayed with it because I really enjoy what I do."

Tennis Equipment Design Today

The beauty of tennis is that it can be played by almost everyone all over the world. Children as young as five and seniors in their 70s and 80s have been known to lob the ball right over the net or volley competitively for the next point. The game has existed for hundreds of years and can be played inside or out. The game is fun, because every court, every racquet, every ball, and the weather conditions affect how the game is played. It is challenging and complex and requires different skills at varying times in the game. Even the pros have difficulty gaining equal mastery over every shot.

If tennis is your passion, as an engineer, you can design racquets, strings, balls, and other new equipment to advance the game and reduce injuries. Every year, manufacturers come out with multiple racquet designs to make the game better for the professionals and more enjoyable for the recreational players. String materials made from cow gut to synthetics are designed to give more power or greater control, and more than 70 million tennis balls are manufactured and sold in stores every year. There is a wealth of opportunity in the tennis industry.

Tennis Balls

In tennis, ball design is a complex subject. For tournament play, different court surfaces determine the type of ball that will be used. Grass courts such as Wimbledon are the fastest, closely followed by hard, green clay and red clay courts. Grass courts are considered fast because the surface creates little friction. Clay courts are slow because the surface creates more friction. Most of us have not played on a grass court, but try hitting the ball back and forth in a grass field the next time you play tennis and notice the difference it makes!

Balls are also classified as fast, medium, or slow. An important consideration for ball speed is the height and type of fabric on the outside. Balls with more fuzz have more air resistance, travel more slowly, and, in rainy conditions, the cover material fluffs and further slows the game. Serious players use different felt thicknesses in different altitudes to increase or decrease the air resistance. If the felt thickness changes in the middle of the game from intense volleying or wear, the ball will go faster too.

Professional players can hit serves as fast as 135 mph. When a ball is hit with that much force, an engineer must understand what happens during the impact. How does the ball deform and how does that affect its resulting performance characteristics? After considerable deformation, can the ball be used the next day? Will it offer the same spin ability or, more important, will it impact the present match?

To answer some of these questions, the United States Tennis Association (USTA) uses a Stevens machine to compress the tennis balls. Each ball is squash-tested, or compressed, for 10 seconds and then checked for deformation. If the ball does not return to a round shape, it is rejected by the USTA.

Engineers often test tennis ball aerodynamics in a wind tunnel, which blows air over the tennis ball to determine how the forces act on it. For example, if the tunnel blows air over the tennis ball at 135 mph, it simulates a ball served at 135 mph. Wind tunnels are fascinating and provide the engineer with important aerodynamic data that would be close to impossible to obtain any other way.

According to Penn, a tennis ball begins its life as a mound of powder that forms the core. The type of play the ball is made for determines the ingredients in the core. For example, the extended-life ball has titanium mixed into the powder to allow it to last longer. The beginner's ball has a softer core, to allow the ball to stay in play longer and give the player more control.

The powder is shaped into pellets and placed in a mold that makes half of the ball. Two halves are glued together, or fused, and a machine injects one atmosphere of air pressure. Finally, the ball cover, made of nylon, cotton felt, and wool, is bonded to the core. The balls are then packaged and shipped to the stores.

To understand the basic physics of tennis and to learn how speed, spin, height, and altitude determine the flight of a tennis ball, visit http://wings.avkids.com. This interactive software program is part of the Aeronautics Internet Textbook and offers a wealth of information on all things aeronautical, from tennis ball trajectories to careers that use aeronautics.

Tennis Racquets

To a person who doesn't play tennis, a racquet is a device to hit a tennis ball over the net. To a tennis racquet designer, a tennis racquet is a work of art that presents a constant challenge in creating the "perfect" racquet for each level of player ability. Many years ago, the average racquet weighed two to three pounds. A few years ago, the average racquet weighed 11–12 ounces. Today, racquets made with high-tech alloys weigh only seven or eight ounces. What do you think happens to the player and to the game when the weight is lowered or redistributed? More mass or weight usually equals more power. How would you maintain the power of a stroke despite a lower racquet weight?

The answer to the problem lies in determining the correct string tension. The strings on a racquet are another feat of science and engineering in racquet design. By changing the position of the strings or by designing different string geometry configurations, the "sweet spot" can be enlarged and more power can be delivered to off-center hits. An average or low-strength player can still whack the ball proficiently with a well-designed racket.

Another approach engineers have considered involves larger racquet heads that make it easier to hit the ball. When Howard Head took up tennis in the 1970s, he created a racquet with a string surface area that was almost double the surface area of other wooden racquets in use at that time. When the increased surface area made the racquet too heavy, Head developed a lightweight aluminum frame. The new racquet changed the face of tennis forever, as millions of tennis players bought the

> Today, because of all the advances in materials design and the constant search for more speed on the court, the International Tennis Federation has constrained the size of a racquet head to 135 square inches. This standard allows no competitor an unfair advantage.

larger, yet lighter, racquets in the hopes of beating their opponent. Other engineers, in their quest to keep up with technological advances in tennis racquet design, put liquid in the frame for added weight on swings and added other materials under the grips and in the handles to reduce vibrations. Do you have a different idea for lowering the weight and maintaining the power of the racquet? There are many opportunities for the creative engineer in the tennis industry.

A good racquet design should also reduce a player's susceptibility to injuries such as tennis elbow and other arm injuries that are caused by

This tennis raquet by Head is made of lightweight magnesium.

vibrations from hitting the ball. Injuries produced from a badly hit ball and poor grip are painful, uncomfortable, and take away the fun of the game. Tennis racquet engineers have the ability to make a difference in the lives of many people.

Engineers who do this:

- **Aeronautical/Aerospace Engineers**—May design tennis balls and/or racquets and research the aerodynamics of tennis play.
- **Civil Engineers**—May design courts and other tennis venues.
- **Materials Engineers**—May look for new materials to make the game more fun or challenging, such as racquet components (e.g., strings and grips) or balls (cores and cover materials), and may work with civil engineers to design new court surfaces that reduce injury while also slowing or speeding up the game.
- **Mechanical Engineers**—May design tennis racquets or the machines that produce them, or be involved in the manufacturing processes of racquets, ball launchers, or line-call systems that determine whether a ball is hit in or out of play.

Tennis-related companies that hire engineers:

- Dunlop Sports—www.dunlopsports.com
- Head—www.head.com
- Penn—www.penn.com
- Prince—www.princetennis.com
- ProKennex—www.prokennex.com
- Volkl—www.volkl.com
- Wilson—www.wilsonsports.com

More resources:

- Aeronautics Internet Textbook—http://wings.avkids.com
- International Sports Engineering Association—www.sports-engineering.co.uk
- International Tennis Federation—www.itftennis.com
- Raquet Research—www.racquetresearch.com
- Tennis Server—www.tennisserver.com
- United States Tennis Association—www.usta.com
- United States Racquet Stringers Association—www.tennisone.com

INLINE SKATING

Jamie Page, Mechanical Engineer
and Founder of Crosskate

"I've been athletic my entire life. I love to mountain bike and ski. I grew up in Massachusetts and always had ideas for cool new products that were not available. I decided to become an engineer, because I saw it as the best way to invent things. I earned a mechanical engineering degree from MIT and later moved to California to attend grad school at Stanford. Although I missed the snow, I was amazed by the fantastic dirt-packed hiking, biking, and walking trails in California. I kept thinking, it would be so much fun if I could somehow practice skiing on them.

"At the time, I had just started a product development firm called Underground Design. We focused on designing medical devices, toys, and sporting goods. The inspiration for the prototype design for Crosskate came during an overnight bus trip in India. I wanted to cross the principles of roller skating, skiing, and mountain biking, but I didn't know if it would work.

"I made the prototype using two-by-fours and lawnmower wheels and entered the Crosskate business plan in the $50K Entrepreneurship Competition at MIT. It came in second place! The award carried a $10,000 prize, networking opportunities, and the ability to get serious about my invention.

"The original tires came from a used handcart. The steering mechanism was the most difficult hurdle, followed by the braking system. Only after many, many attempts, during which we kept learning and learning, did we get the mechanism designed. Now the front tire doesn't roll backward, so you can climb. We had to design a special bearing with a one-way mechanism built in.

"Crosskate went into production in the summer of 2000 and we now have several ski resorts that will be renting the skates for use on their mountains in the summer. Without my background in engineering, none of this would be possible!"

Skate Equipment Design Today

Inline skating is an extremely popular participant sport worldwide. In 1996, 31 million people participated in the sport, and today the numbers are even higher. The beauty of skating is that whether you are using skates for transportation, playing hockey or basketball, dancing, fitness, or sailing with the wind across empty lots, you have the ability to thoroughly express and enjoy yourself.

This enjoyment is expanded and increased by having the proper equipment such as knee and wrist pads, a helmet, and well-maintained skates. Engineers are at the forefront of making the sport safer and more fun by applying engineering principles to create the wheels, bearings, frames, boots, and safety gear. (For more information about designing the helmet and other protective gear, check out the Helmets chapter.)

The creation of an inline skate is no small feat of engineering. For example, just to create the wheels of a skate, engineers go through meticulous design and testing phases that depend on the type of skating an individual wants. An aggressive skater wants speed and maneuverability. Recreational skaters need comfort and stability. Fitness enthusiasts desire a good low-impact and cardiovascular workout. Inline racers want precision engineering for maximum speed and, as explained in Jamie Page's profile above, some want to traverse mountains in the quest for the ultimate trail or activity. There are unlimited possibilities for the engineer with an interest in skating and a creative streak to take skate design to the next level.

Aggressive skaters can defy gravity by performing flips, skating on ramps, sliding on rails, grinding, and other challenging stunts.

Because aggressive skating is riskier, diverse, and expressive, it requires the most rugged gear to protect against unforeseen consequences. The engineer rarely knows what types of new stunts will be tried by thrill-seeking skaters. The engineers in this industry must strive to meet the challenge of helping skaters reach new levels of performance while ensuring that the equipment can endure the pounding that it takes day after day from riders with a wide variety of body types and skating styles.

So what does it take to engineer a wheel for the inline skater? To give some background on inline skate wheels, most are made of polyurethane. They are classified by:

- Diameter or wheel size: They range from 43 mm to 80 mm. In general, taller wheels are less maneuverable but go faster than shorter wheels. Taller wheels last longer and are more expensive than shorter wheels. Larger wheels are also better for rough terrain.

- Hardness or durometer number: The durometer number is between 0 and 100, with 100 being the hardest. A wheel with a lower  durometer number is usually good for skating outdoors, where the surfaces are generally bumpy. The softer wheels act as a shock absorber and allow the skater to cruise more comfortably. Harder wheels perform well on smooth surfaces such as skating rinks and allow for a faster ride. Aggressive skaters may even swap wheels with different durometer numbers depending on the weather conditions. The tradeoff of low vs. high durometer numbers is that the softer wheels (lower durometer numbers) are less expensive and provide better shock absorption but will wear out faster. Harder wheels are more expensive, offer a smoother and faster ride, and last longer.

- Hubs or cores: The hubs hold the bearings and are defined as everything except the wheel material. Wheels can have open or closed hubs. They are critical to performance, because imperfections can cause misalignments. Misalignments cause friction and drag that produce heat and eventually destroy the wheel.

- Profile: The profile refers to how skinny or fat the wheels are and determines how much traction the wheels get. Aggressive skaters who want to pivot quickly and take off fast require a larger footprint or profile. Although the skates don't go as fast, they increase maneuverability. Inline racers, on the other hand, want a slimmer profile to go faster and, thereby, sacrifice stability for speed.

Engineers also need to understand wheel bearings. Bearings are typically sealed (no maintenance, most protective, and expensive) or shielded (most common and can shield the inside from dirt and debris, although they are not watertight). Recreational bearings usually come filled with grease. High-performance bearings that provide less fiction typically have a pop-out cap, so the bearings can be cleaned and maintained.

Bearings are rated on the ABEC (Annular Bearing Engineering Committee) of the American Bearing Manufacturing Association scale. A higher ABEC rating or number means that the bearing was manufactured with greater precision and will result in lower friction. Lower friction usually means faster skating, but often, the miniscule changes in speed achieved by precisely engineering the bearings will affect only the professional who may be trying to shave a few tenths of a second off an already fast time.

Most retail inline skates use micro-bearings or 688 bearings. They come greased for extended wear with little maintenance needed. However, when performance is an issue, get shielded bearings that can be cleaned and relubricated when they stop spinning well. Some skates enable the owner to replace or swap bearings when changing from aggressive to recreational skating or from speed skating to inline hockey.

Whatever your passion, as an engineer in the skating industry, you can also work on speed skates, hockey skates, ice skates, and others that have all recently been re-engineered. The skating industry is sure to be challenging, as new forms of skating hit the streets and new materials for bearings, wheels, boots, and frames become more readily available.

Engineers who do this:

- **Civil Engineers**—May design skate parks that allow skaters to jump benches, slide down poles, maneuver over ledges, and/or invent other obstacles that allow skaters to do tricks; may design portable ramps and ledges for learning to do tricks at home or to allow skaters to set up a makeshift park anywhere they want.
- **Manufacturing Engineers**—Determine systems to get skates manufactured and are interested in reducing the costs associated with production.
- **Materials Engineers**—May look for new materials to have more fun and provide a better ride (boots, wheels, bearings, frames, hubs, and everything else).
- **Mechanical Engineers**—design the frames, wheels, bearings, and everything in between.

Inline Skate-related companies that hire engineers:
- K2 Skates—www.k2sports.com
- Oxygen—www.oxygenskates.com
- Rollerblade—www.rollerblade.com
- Salomon—www.salomonsports.com
- Ultra Wheels—www.ultrawheels.com
- V-Line Skate Company—www.vlineskate.com

More resources:
- Aggressive Skaters Association—www.asaskate.com
- American National Standards Institute (ANSI)—www.ansi.org
- American Society For Testing And Materials (ASTM)—www.astm.org
- Bicycle Helmet Safety Institute (BHSI)—www.bhsi.org
- National Inline Basketball League—www.nysol.com
- National Safe Kids Campaign—www.safekids.org
- Protective Headgear Manufacturer's Association (PHMA)—www.phma.org
- USA Hockey Inline—www.usahockey.com
- USA Roller Sports —www.usarollersports.org
- U.S. Consumer Product Safety Commission (CPSC)—www.cpsc.gov

FISHING

John Chapman, EIT,
Director of Spinning Reel Development, Pure Fishing

"From a young age, I enjoyed working with mechanical items. My father and I worked on many mechanical projects, and, at times, I took apart more than I could put back together. My parents were very supportive and helped me to enroll in the mechanical engineering program at the University of Missouri at Rolla (UMR).

"Because I didn't apply myself to any great extent in high school, I had to work very hard in my college math courses. I remember my Introduction to Engineering professor saying that only one out of 10 of us would graduate. The statement startled me into action. I worked very hard, and achievement became a competition between my roommates and me. I did not believe they were any smarter, so I had to be able to succeed. This competitive spirit carried me through the program.

"All my life I have loved to fish. I remember spending many afternoons on the riverbank waiting for the "the big one" to take my line. My parents were encouraging, because they offered to clean anything I could bring home. I was allowed to have all the fun without the hard work.

"When I graduated from UMR I began to work at Ericsson Lightwave in fiber optics until the day my wife found an ad in the paper from Berkley for a fishing rod design engineer. It was the perfect opportunity to combine my love of engineering and fishing into a career that could enhance the sport. I got the job and have been working in the fishing industry for the last 17 years.

"At Pure Fishing, I am responsible for creating new spinning and spin cast fishing reels. I watch new technologies, materials, or processing techniques that might have application to our products. I also review old patents for ideas that might have been great but had poor timing. I am on the constant search to add new features, new looks, or performance criteria to enhance new or existing designs.

"The new product process has several routes, but we always work toward developing high-impact styling, superior features that outpace the competition, and performance benefits that enhance the sport. We utilize a 3D CAD (Computer Aided Design) system to design our products. We definitely put effort into styling; this is what initially attracts our customer. The most functional reel in the world will not sell if it doesn't look good, too. We then put our efforts into making certain the product functions exceptionally well and will continue to work.

"I definitely enjoy my work, because I can personally relate to the use of the products. The great thing about being an engineer in this industry is that after a prototype is created, I do my best to test it on a beautiful stretch of water. It is very satisfying to know that the products you are working with will provide many people with future enjoyment in the great sport of fishing."

Fishing Equipment Design Today

To the avid angler, nothing is better than a beautiful river or lake, high-tech fishing equipment, perfect weather, and the promise of fish in the water. The lure of what may be caught has been paramount in the minds of fishing enthusiasts since the beginning. But fishing equipment has come a long way from the cane pole setups of yesterday to the carbon-fiber, vibration-dampening poles of today. Engineers in this industry apply their engineering skills to keep the big one from getting away. The technology behind fishing can provide an interesting career for an individual interested in both fishing and engineering.

When we think about fishing, most of us don't think about all the technology that goes into creating the perfect pole, guides, reel seats, handles, and reels. Catching a 175-pound marlin off of a fishing boat in high-rolling waves requires very different equipment than catching a five-pound salmon while standing on a riverbank. Big fish require equipment to absorb some shock so that the line, guides, and pole do not break. The line should be a heavy test line that has the ability to stretch. The rod should be a slow action rod to further absorb the shock.

One look at the different rods and reels available at a fishing supply store can boggle the mind. Rods for every type of fish, style, or technique of fishing and weather condition are available. Rods are made of plastic, carbon fiber, graphite, and bamboo. The fishing rod, itself, (without the reel and guides) is called a blank. The reel seats, which secure the reel to the blank, are designed for fresh or salt water and are specific to spinning, fly-fishing, or baitcasting. They come with or without triggers, cushions, or with holes in the middle and can be made of composites or metal. Even the fishing line is elastic or not.

The engineers who design blanks rate them for stiffness based on the blank's curvature under constant tension. The blanks vary in length and in composition of materials. As a general rule, a heavy action rod is stiffer and will help to catch heavy, strong, or medium-size fish in heavy currents. A light action rod is great for peaceful days on a dock, with essentially no current, to catch sunfish or perch.

Another rod characteristic is the action. Blanks can be extra fast, fast, medium, or slow. A fast action rod works well for powerful fish because the pole is very stiff and resists powerful fish. In a fast action pole, only the two or three feet at its tip will bend to absorb the shock of a struggling fish. In contrast, a slow or soft action blank is very sensitive and flexible. Practically the entire pole bends when the fish takes a bite and tries to escape. The eyes of beginning fishing enthusiasts who use such poles light up in excitement as they watch their pole bend in half when a tiny fish shows up for breakfast or lunch.

The real challenge for engineers in this industry is designing gear for the unlimited possibilities of fishing conditions and species of fish. So, a person in pursuit of fish will need a wide variety of fishing poles, otherwise that person will have to fish in the same spot, in the same conditions, and eat the same type of fish every day.

Aside from rod and reel design, engineers are also hard at work creating all the electronics that can help catch the big one. Designing and testing GPS systems, fish finders, and navigation plotters are examples of the engineering employment possibilities.

If you have ever spent the day fishing and barely received a nibble, you will appreciate having the ability simply to know where the fish are, so that you can cast your line in the right spot and perhaps enjoy more success or have more fun. An example of highly sophisticated electronics for fishing is the fish finder. Fish finders work by sending sound waves through the water. This sound travels at 4,800 feet per second through water. For the sonar to detect a fish, it sends the signal, the signal bounces off a fish, and a computer measures the time it takes for the signal to return. The signals that return in less time show fish that are closer to your boat. The signals that take longer to return show fish that are closer to the bottom or maybe the bottom itself, which is also useful, to help you avoid running aground.

Companies that produce the electronics for the fishing industry usually hire electrical, mechanical, quality, test, and software engineers. To create a fish finder, engineers determine the proper frequency, cone angle (a wider angled cone scans more water), the type of transducer, and transducer mount (how it attaches to the boat) to send the sound waves through the water. The frequency for fresh water will be different than for salt water. Shallow water will require a different frequency than deep water. Even water with a strong current will require a different frequency than water with no current.

The fish finder display is also a work of art for the engineer. Many years ago the display was black and white, and there was a delay in the picture. The fish would be gone by the time the display showed it was there. The first-generation color displays also presented problems, because it was very hard to see the colors in the sunlight, because sunlight contains the same colors that were used on the display. The colors of a rainbow are red, orange, yellow, green, blue, indigo, and violet. In the presence of sunlight, the rainbow colors effectively canceled out the same color in the display. Today, however, engineers have designed color screens with improved resolution and have increased the computer processing power, which has eliminated the delay.

The important thing that a future engineer must realize is that engineering is an evolutionary process. To use the fish finder as an example, early designs were in black and white. Engineers went back to work on an already useful and popular product to make it better. They added color screens, wider cone angles, and better transducers. The finder was now far more sophisticated and selling better than ever before, but engineers still went back to work on it to make it even better. The fish finders of today have even more processing power, can tell the exact size of a fish, and can even differentiate varying bottom terrains. You know that, as you read this, engineers still are hard at work revamping the fish finder design. What's next? How would you improve the design?

Engineers who do this:

- **Chemical and Materials Engineers**—May develop or design rods, reels, reel seats, grips, guide set, or materials that will be stronger, make fishing more fun, or increase the sensitivity to fish bites.
- **Electrical, Test, Quality, and Software Engineers**—May design fish finders, GPS systems, or fishing information systems.
- **Manufacturing Engineers**—May design systems or processes for manufacturing anything in the fishing industry such as rods, reels, flies, hooks, and fishing electronics.
- **Mechanical Engineers**—May design rods and reels, reel seats, grips, guide sets, or the manufacturing processes.

Fishing-related companies that hire engineers:

- Fenwick—www.fenwickfishing.com
- House of Hardy—www.houseofhardy.com
- G Loomis—www.loomis.com
- Lowrance—www.lowrance.com
- Orvis—www.orvis.com
- Penn—www.penn.com
- Pinnacle—www.pinnacle.com
- Quantum—www.quantum.com
- Shimano—www.shimano.com
- Zebco—www.zebco.com

More resources:

- Fenwick—Rod Science—www.fenwickfishing.com
- House of Hardy—How a Reel is Made—www.hardyfishing.com
- Pure Fishing—www.purefishing.com

BASEBALL AND FOOTBALL

Mark McNamee, EIT,
Bat Research and Development Engineer, Easton

"As a kid, I always wanted to know how and why things worked. My dad had books on the physics of baseball, and I found myself captivated by the sections on why curve balls curve and what makes the ball spin. The game of baseball has always been a passion of mine as a player, coach, fan, and student of the game.

"I went to University of California at Davis for a mechanical engineering degree, because it seemed really challenging and I knew it would open the most doors for my future. Because of my interest in sports and the human body, I focused my electives on anatomy (physiology) and biomechanics. After college, I briefly worked for a medical device company but found that I wanted something more tangible, exciting, and aligned with my hobby.

"Since baseball was such a big part of my life, I contacted Easton (my first choice) and captured a position as a bat engineer.

"As a bat engineer, I am constantly on the lookout for materials and innovations that will make bats better. I focus primarily on testing the bats quantitatively and qualitatively for:

- Performance—We use a swing robot to test bats for impact, speed, and "sweet spot."
- Durability—We use a cannon that fires the balls into the bat at speeds up to 160 mph, 1,000 times to simulate two to three years of rugged use.
- Feel—We measure the sting, weight, and balance.

"Baseball bats are a competitive market. Each year at Easton, we look at bats that are already on the market and try to invent new features to improve their design. In addition, we work hard to develop new materials for new bat designs that will make our bats outshine the competition or fill a need for the athlete.

"One of the best things about my job is that I often test the bats myself. We have a batting cage here at Easton that I use two to four times a week when developing a new bat. Occasionally, we also bring in ex-professional and college players for additional testing purposes. Without my strong background in baseball, I wouldn't really understand if the bat I designed was appropriate for its intended use.

"Today, I play semi-pro baseball, and it is really fun to be able to use a bat that I developed. However, even better than that is the sense of pride and accomplishment that I feel from developing products that are in the stores and giving many people countless hours of entertainment and enjoyment. It's fun to go to work every day, because I am doing something that I love. Without my engineering degree, none of this would be possible."

Baseball Equipment Design Today

When a batter walks up to the plate and the crowd goes wild, all eyes and attention alternate between the batter and bat, and the pitcher and ball. The ball, thrown at 90–100 mph, crosses the plate in about a half-second. The batter has a quarter-second to determine if the pitcher has thrown a ball or a strike. That's a quarter-second to determine where the ball will cross the plate. Only a quarter-second determines if the batter goes down in history or simply goes back to the dugout. If the batter swings and makes contact with the ball, the crack of the bat, that famous home run sound, generates almost 16,000 pounds of force in the bat handle.

In all this excitement, little thought is given to the engineers behind the scenes who improve the bats, the baseballs, the gloves, and the technology that tells how far the ball was hit. The engineers behind the scenes are dynamic, creative, and hardworking folks who have revolutionized the way the game is played.

One major revolution in bat technology comes from Active Control Systems (ACX). The bat "sweet spot" is a location on the bat that, when hit, allows for maximum power and minimum vibration.

Usually this spot is about five to six inches from the end of the bat. If the ball misses the "sweet spot" it will not go as far, and the resulting vibration will create an uncomfortable sting in the batter's hands. ACX developed a piezoelectric dampener that, when placed in a metal bat, transforms the vibration to electric energy that dissipates out of the end of the bat as heat. This bat, although illegal for professional games (only the amateurs get to play with space-age equipment, because metal bats are not allowed), has accelerated the learning curve of Little League players and other amateur players of all ages. Other high-tech bats are made from graphite, titanium, and ceramic.

An important consideration for all engineers who design baseball equipment involves determining how to make the game safer. Although baseball is one of the safest games played, according to the NCAA Injury Surveillance System (ISS), higher performance equipment also means harder hits, faster flying balls, and the possibility of an increasing number of injuries. The highest risk of injury comes from the impact of a baseball with a player. In the U.S., from 1973-1995, 88 children between the ages of 5 and 14 died from injuries while playing baseball, softball, and t-ball.

One of the best things about being a baseball equipment engineer is the opportunity to help reverse this trend, through developing new technology. To make baseball safer, many engineers continually work on developing new materials that will make the ball softer or helmets harder for youth play. Once a new ball or helmet is designed or created, other engineers test the impact forces and injury-reducing performance or potential.

On the other side of the coin is player support of new materials. For example, when a new major-league ball was introduced, 931 home runs were hit in the month of April 2000, alone. Pitchers blamed the high number of home runs on the ball, insisting that it was "juiced." "If the new balls were juiced, the coefficient of restitution (COR) test would show it," said Sandy Alderson, spokesman for Major League Baseball. Each ball is made by hand, measured, weighed, and checked for 17 different types of defects. Balls that make the cut are sent to the major leagues, and the ones that don't are sold on the retail market.

So, what happened to increase the home runs so dramatically? Scientists and the baseball manufacturer, Rawlings Sporting Goods, insisted that the new ball was identical to the old ball in all areas of testing, the methods deemed appropriate by the American Society of Testing Materials (including testing the COR). The tests showed that all balls fell into the major league's required specifications and that there were no significant differences in the performance or durability.

The new balls, however, had a lower stitch height, which lessened the pitcher's grip on the ball (curve balls curve less with less stitch height), making the pitch more favorable for the batter. Engineers in this industry, therefore, need to be very aware of the psychological and nontesting impact of their prod- ucts. When an engineer designs for  people, and money and careers are at stake, a slight and seemingly miniscule change in materials can have a major and long-lasting impact on a player or the game as a whole.

Football Equipment Design Today

Football design illustrates another important aspect of engineering: The engineering design process is more of a journey than a destination. Every year, engineers go back to work to create the perfect design. What was per- fect last year may not seem so perfect this year, and what was popular a few years ago may be obsolete now. In addition, engineers and scientists develop new materials with new applications every day and, from time to time, can create vast improvements in a current design.

The first football game was played at Rutgers University in New Jersey on November 6, 1869. At the time, the ball was round, and forward pass- ing was illegal. In 1912, the ball became shaped more like a watermelon, and, in 1935, the current shape was adopted. In the early days of the game, a common problem was that the ball would become deflated in the middle of a game and players had to take turns blowing it up, a process that could take 30 minutes. Soon, engineers at Wilson Sporting Goods invented a valve-inflated football that significantly lowered the possibil- ity that the ball would deflate and, at the same time, reduced inflation time to only five minutes.

Today, in each NFL game, each team receives 48 new footballs for outdoor games and 36 for indoor games. The balls must be available for the referee to test with a pressure gauge before the game. Twelve are sealed in a special box, can only be handled by the referee, and are marked with a "K" for the kickers. In the NFL, a new ball must be used for every kick, to keep kickers from using a doctored ball that may give them an advantage.

Footballs are created by cutting four leather panels, hand sewing the panels together, inserting a bladder, and then overinflating it to check for defects or inconsistencies in craftsmanship. In addition, before the panels are sewn together, each is weighed and checked for discoloration or imperfections. A regulation football is 11 inches long and 28 inches around its widest point.

Today, even more research techniques are employed to understand the game and the ramifications of advances in technology. For example, a researcher at the University of Buffalo is trying to find out why a forward pass of a football travels to the right or the left. Using wind tunnel testing and high-speed photography, this researcher may uncover data that can change the way footballs are designed. Other researchers seek to determine the perfect angle and place to kick the ball that will lead to the highest velocity or speed when the ball leaves the foot. Still other researchers may always be on the lookout for new materials to decrease the weight and/or increase the impact resistance of a football player's shoulder, neck, jaw, hip, thigh, or knee padding.

If an engineering career in the football or baseball industry grabs your attention, be sure to read the chapters on helmet design and broadcast engineering for even more careers in this industry.

Engineers who do this:

- **Biomedical Engineers**—May research the impact aspects of baseball and football to determine the padding requirements.
- **Chemical and Materials Engineers**—May work to develop or design new lightweight materials for headgear that will be more comfortable and withstand greater impacts or forces or develop new pills and windings for the internals of baseballs or covers and strings for the outside.
- **Computer/Software Engineers**—May design software or hardware to aid in pressure or impact detection analysis, manufacturing processes, or information systems, as well as design systems to obtain faster analysis of plays, such as grid mapping stadiums to determine how far a ball was hit within seconds of its landing.
- **Manufacturing Engineers**—May design systems or processes for manufacturing ball materials or bats more efficiently.
- **Mechanical Engineers**—May design pitching machines; new bat, ball, or helmet testing methods; and systems for manufacturing, motion analysis or impact testing, as well as be involved in building and testing prototypes.

Baseball- and football-related companies that hire engineers:

- Demarini Sports—www.demarini.com
- DuPont—www.dupont.com
- Riddell—www.riddell.com
- Spaulding Sporting Goods—www.spaulding.com
- Wilson Sporting Goods—www.wilsonsports.com
- Worth—www.worthsports.com

More resources:

- How NFL Equipment Works—www.howstuffworks.com
- International Sports Engineering Association—www.sports-engineering.co.uk
- The Science of Baseball—www.exploratorium.edu/baseball
- The "Unofficial" Method for Baseball Design—www.worthsports.com

SNOW SPORTS

Stacie Glass,
former Snowboard Design Engineer, K2 Snowboards

"When I was a kid, we called my grandfather 'Fix-it Grandpa.' He could fix anything, and I often followed him around asking questions about everything. I was always fascinated when he took everything apart; only, if I did it, I couldn't always get it back together. Neither of my parents were mechanically inclined, so, when I needed something fixed, I either had to call Grandpa or fix it myself.

"When I was graduating from high school, I wanted to go to college at University of California, Santa Barbara. My dad and I were looking through the college catalog and ran across a picture of a Human Powered Vehicle under the mechanical engineering section.

We both agreed that it looked interesting, and I felt confident that I could study mechanical engineering, because I enjoyed math, science, and physics. I signed up, and it was the hardest, but also the most rewarding, thing that I have ever done. Because of my engineering education, I feel that I can solve any problem and can do whatever I want with my life. The education gave me a set of tools to have a successful life.

"Throughout school, I was vice-president of Pi Tau Sigma, a mechanical engineering honor society, the Web site administrator for the Society of Women Engineers (SWE), a member of the American Society of Mechanical Engineers (ASME), and I won the grand prize in the Institute of Electrical and Electronics Engineers, Inc. (IEEE) Web Page Design Contest. To make extra money, I worked for Joyride

Snowboards as a college sales rep. I had been an avid snowboarder for the last 12 years so it seemed like a good fit to use my engineering skills to further the sport of snowboarding.

"My employment at K2 started as an internship after graduation and eventually became a full-time gig. At K2, I designed snowboard footprints, profiles, and constructions with an emphasis on women's boards. I also organized and led on-snow tests on Mt. Hood for prototype testing. My design, the K2 Mix, is still in production and was ranked in the Top 5 Women's boards in the 2002 Transworld Buyers Guide. In fact, Gretchen Bleiler, the winner of the Women's Superpipe in the 2003 X-Games and the Women's US Open Halfpipe Championships rides my board!"

Skiing, Snowboarding, and Skeleton Equipment Design Today

Do you remember the last time you saw the downhill ski competition in the Olympics? What about ski jumping, speed skating, skeleton racing, bobsledding, figure skating, or snowboarding? What do all of these have in common? Cold weather sports and engineering! For millions of adrenaline junkies, the onset of winter is pure elation. As the slopes get covered in snow, the rush of flying down a mountain at 70 mph to 80 mph satisfies even the most demanding endorphin-seeking hedonists. Do you remember watching the skis or boards scream right through all that powder or watching in horror as the ice-packed snow defeated a contestant, who went toppling down a hill at bone-breaking speeds?

What if you could make a difference in the performance of the participants in the Olympic games? What if you could improve a skier's performance—making her go faster, turn sharper, jump higher, or simply feel better? What if you could create a sports product that allowed professionals to break the current world records? What if you could enable snowboarders to take a turn at 3 Gs? What if you could decrease a snow-lover's susceptibility to injury? If that sounds like something you would like to do, it's time to wake up and get ready for your career. That's exactly what engineers in this industry do every day.

Skis and Snowboards

Engineers who love to ski and snowboard naturally gravitate toward work in the snow sports industry. Traditionally, when an idea for a new ski or snowboard design came along, engineers would build a proto-type, perform laboratory tests for stiffness, and test it on the slopes. Based on the test experience, engineers would make design changes and retest the equipment. This method of design resulted in a slow and tedious process. In addition, the perfectly crafted ski or snowboard is not perfect for everyone. The needs of a 5'2" female snowboarder are much different than the needs of a 6'0" male snowboarder. The snow-boarder's height, weight, and skill level, as well as the snow conditions and the angle of the slope, all need to be taken into consideration when trying to fit the perfect board to the enthusiast.

Snowboards are made out of several layers of materials, along with glue and paint. Snowboarders believe that the edge design, or effective edge, is the most important part of the design. The edge refers to the edge around the board. Edge design determines how the snowboard will turn. The more surface area the edge has, the more control, and, hence, the sharper the turns that can be made. Riders can find a chart that cross-references their height and weight to a certain board length. Generally, tall people should have longer boards.

Structural strength of the snowboard is also very important. Engineers determine the strength by figuring out the acceleration of the rider. Acceleration is determined by finding the coefficient of friction, the incline plane, and the combined mass of the rider and board. On fresh fluffy snow, a heavier boarder on a short board will cut deeper into the snow and reduce the speed. On a long board, the edges may not stay in contact with the snow at all for a light person. If the edges don't stay in contact, this results in a loss of control and reduced speeds. In general, a narrow snowboard allows for turning control, and a wide snowboard goes faster.

Ski designs vary with different environmental conditions. Longer skis provide more stability and allow for more control at higher speeds, while shorter skis turn better in any conditions, because there is less ski to manage. However, shorter skis may also vibrate at high speeds, which causes a loss of control. Wider skis distribute the rider's weight over a larger area and are, therefore, better for soft, powdery snow. To ski on hard-packed snow, a rider wants an hourglass ski that digs deeper and makes sharper cuts.

To accommodate these various environmental conditions, engineers from manufacturers such as K2 and Head are designing intelligent technology that will enable skiers and snowboarders to go faster and have more control. K2 is using piezoelectric devices (special sensors) to detect vibration and act like a shock absorber to get rid of the

vibration. The sensors act like the human body's nerve endings in sensing shock but also absorb vibration and convert the shock or vibration into an electrical charge. A tiny control circuit then releases the energy through heat, which eliminates the vibrations. With less vibration, skiers can better control their rides and can go faster and make quicker turns. Also, with reduced vibrations, more of the ski stays in contact with the snow and the end result is greater stability, higher speeds, and smoother riding.

Head is using Intellifibers to do almost the same thing. The board is preset for fluffy or softer snow. When the rider encounters a hard-packed or icy area, the Intellifibers reduce vibration by converting the mechanical energy to electric energy that automatically stiffens the board.

A driver has optimum control over a car, for example, when all four tires are on the road. Similarly, in skiing or snowboarding, optimum control requires that the entire ski or snowboard edge be in contact with the snow at all times. If a car turns very fast and two tires leave the road, the driver loses control and probably begins to wonder whether the car will flip or hit an object in its path. Vibration that causes a ski or snowboard edge to come off the snow usually has the same effect, making the skier wonder whether he is going to flip or hit objects in his path. A professional race car has very wide tires to provide more traction and keep the driver in full control at the fastest possible speed. The same theory holds true for snowboarders and skiers, who have the most control when the entire surface area of the ski or board is touching the snow.

Currently, this same dampening technology is also being used in other sports equipment such as baseball bats, golf clubs, fishing poles, water skis, and mountain bikes. Any sport you can think of where less vibration would increase performance is a market for this technology.

SKELETON RACING

"A margin of victory of 1/100 second is not uncommon, the second place finisher often having lost crucial time by not maintaining an aerodynamic position, taking an incorrect line through a turn, or even by barely brushing a shoulder against a concrete wall coming down the course."

Chris Soule
Olympic Skeleton Racer

Skeleton racing is one of the most extreme sports in existence. Athletes jump on a little three-foot-long fiberglass board headfirst, with their face just inches above the ice, and rocket down ice-covered concrete walls at 80 mph. They cover almost a mile with no steering mechanism, no brakes (besides a toe hanging off that also acts as a rudder), and little ability even to see the next turn coming up fast! However, even with these adrenaline-pumping limitations, skeleton racing is known to be one of the safest sports in the Olympics, because of excellent work by engineers!

Photo courtesy International Bobsleigh and Skeleton Federation

Creating the skeleton track is a major feat of engineering. The walls can be no higher than 18 inches, the maximum track gradient is 15% and the curves have to be constructed so that a racer does not exceed a force of 4 Gs (four times the weight of the racer's body) for longer than three seconds. Every element of the design will put some kind of stress on the racers. Engineers must be sensitive to how those forces are applied to the human body.

New bobsled, skeleton, and luge tracks for the winter Olympics take about 16–30 months to complete. Many of those months are spent doing

Photo courtesy International Bobsleigh and Skeleton Federation

computer simulations of the track design. Engineers make sure that the track is challenging and then check it for safety. Engineers have to make sure that the athletes won't get thrown out of the track, no matter where they crash or how fast they are going. The track designed in Italy for the 2006 Olympics is 1,435 meters long and consists of 19 curves, as well as a vertical drop of 114 meters.

The first rule in skeleton racing is that the more the racer manipulates the control of her sled, the slower she goes. According to Olympic champion Chris Soule, "Driving a sled through a course consists of finding a line that will minimize collisions with the concrete walls, maximize acceleration out of curves, and avoid fishtailing and skidding on the straightaways. Often the fastest sled appears to slingshot cleanly out of every turn while traveling the natural high and low points of the curves and following the path of least resistance throughout the course."

Skeleton racing sleds come in long or short designs or sizes. On the longer design, the racers can have their knees on the sled, whereas on the shorter sled, their knees will hang off. The design chosen is merely a matter of preference. The steel runners that the racers hold onto when running to begin a race must use steel supplied by the Federation Internationale de Bobsleigh et de Tobaganning (FIBT). The bottom of the sled is made to provide jet-like aerodynamic performance. The materials used to create a sled offer both strength and flexibility. The aerospace industry often aids sled designers, because it is one of the few industries that research the properties and resultant effects of materials at low temperatures.

"It is a sport that combines athleticism, aerodynamics, materials technology, physics, and control dynamics all into one," said Great Britain's top men's slider, Kristan Bromley. "The skeleton is an extremely technical piece of equipment that is fine-tuned for each individual track and weather conditions.... The sport, in essence, is about conservation of energy from top to bottom of the track."

Engineers are also employed with racing teams to help them obtain victories. The U.S. National team has tested its sleds in wind tunnels in Buffalo, New York, and Detroit, Michigan, to maximize efficiency. The team also uses high-speed video software to analyze the physics of each corner in a race.

Engineers who do this:

- **Aeronautical/Aerospace Engineers**—May study the aerodynamics of new products (speed, force, drag, and friction analysis are just a few).
- **Biomedical Engineer**—May design systems to analyze the human body while skiing or snowboarding, to aid in injury prevention, or

research the motion of many sports to determine the requirements for product design and keeping people safe.

- **Chemical and Materials Engineers**—May develop or design new lightweight materials that will increase performance, be more comfortable, and withstand greater impacts or forces.
- **Computer/Software Engineers**—May design software or hardware to aid in pressure or impact detection analysis, manufacturing processes, or information systems and design systems or software to allow manufacturers to bring products to market faster.
- **Electrical Engineers**—May design timing systems that ensure the accuracy of the race to 1/1000 of a second.
- **Industrial Engineers**—May maintain bills of materials and routings information and cost standards and recommend pricing for new products, as well as be involved in learning about training others in manufacturing techniques.
- **Manufacturing Engineers**—May design systems or processes for manufacturing skis or snowboards more efficiently.
- **Mechanical Engineers**—May design systems for manufacturing, motion analysis, or impact testing; be involved in building and testing prototypes; and design and develop snow makers.

Snow sports-related companies that hire engineers:
- ACX—www.acx.com
- Burton—www.burton.com
- Head—www.head.com
- K2 Sports—www.k2sports.com

More resources:
- Exploratorium Bobsled Simulator—www.exploratorium.edu
- Federation Internationale de Bobsleigh et de Tobaganning (FIBT) —www.bobsleigh.com
- UC Davis BobSled Simulator—http://mae.engr.ucdavis.edu
- United States Bobsled and Skeleton Federation (USBSF)— www.usabobsledandskeleton.com
- USA Luge—www.usaluge.org
- U.S. Ski Team—www.usskiteam.com

BICYCLING

Georgena Terry,
Founder and CEO of Terry Bicycles

Georgena Terry, after finishing theater and MBA degrees, found that she wasn't satisfied with her life. After taking a vocational test, a counselor recommended that Terry become some kind of engineer. She went back to school and discovered during a design project that she enjoyed brazing and bicycle design. For their project, her group decided to build a hybrid bicycle/car. She learned to braze the bicycle frame from metal tubes, and the rest is history.

Terry wanted to design bicycle frames to reduce riding stress for women. According to Bill Hammack, a chemical engineering professor at the University of Illinois at Urbana-Champaign, "Terry discovered that a woman is not simply a smaller version of a man. For example, a woman's upper body is proportionally longer than a man's upper body. So, a bike that fits a man in the legs and upper body will fit women in only one of those areas. Also, the center of a woman's muscle mass is different than a man's. This means that, when riding a man's bike, a woman's muscles bear more stress. This makes women feel stretched out, giving them neck and shoulder pain. The key to making a woman's bike, she decided, is getting them into a slightly more upright position. Also, she made the handlebars narrower, because a woman's shoulders are not as wide."

If you do what you love, the money will follow. In 1985, Terry's first year in business, she sold 20 of her custom bikes. The next year she sold 1,300 bikes, and the year after that she sold 5,000. Today, Terry Bicycles is a multimillion-dollar company.

Bicycle Equipment Design Today

Bicycling is a favorite sport among the young and the old. The bicycle is the classic example of a simple machine that attracts almost everyone who wants to go faster than walking or skating, with less energy expended. Bicycles have been around since the late 1600s and, through a process of evolution, the innovative engineers who design them are reaching new heights in aerodynamics, performance, propulsion, weight, and durability. Bikes today might weigh just over nine pounds, and recumbent bikes help riders to win races with rocket-like speeds of 81 mph. All-wheel-drive and electric bicycles have hit the market, along with aquacycles that are being used to cross oceans and Xtracycles, with a long backend, that can carry surfboards, lumber, or other loads of up to 200 pounds. There are folding bikes, bikes with brains, bikes with flat-free tires, stationary bikes, and full-metal military bikes. These varied designs all provide creative outlets for bike design and the bicycling engineer.

Engineering bikes involves making them more comfortable, faster, or more fun, depending on the application. Mountain bikers who travel down steep mountains, ride over tree roots, and negotiate hairpin turns on a mountain bike trail have a bumpy ride. When mountain biking became popular, engineers needed to design hard shock absorbers to try to smooth out the ride. Unfortunately, once the shock absorber was set, the rider had to get off the bike to readjust it. If the shock absorber was set for a soft ride (great for going over

those tree roots) it would bottom out under a high-speed impact or when the terrain changed to a small drop-off. If the shock absorber was set in the hard position for heart-pounding riding, the vibration was awful for normal trail riding. Engineers at K2 solved this problem by producing an electric or "smart" shock absorber that uses sensors to automatically adjust the suspension to enhance the performance.

Another example of engineers pushing the envelope to optimize performance is in the materials sector. Optimizing bicycle frame design is a daunting challenge. Different frames are best for different applications and conditions. For example, a mountain bike frame would not be a good choice for a Tour de France bike or a comfort bike. When engineers create frames, they can change the shape or wall thickness of the tubes and use different metals or alloys. Aluminum, titanium, carbon fiber, chromemoly steel, scandium (number 21 on the periodic table—even lighter than titanium), and E5 (a mixture of five other elements in aluminum—also lighter than titanium) are being used to engineer the "perfect" bicycle frame.

When asked about becoming a frame designer, Sean McLaughlin at Specialized Bicycles said, "Working in the bicycle industry can be a great way to merge a personal passion with professional ambition. A lot of us, myself included, feel quite lucky to make a living doing something that we enjoy. Frame design is an exciting area. Technology is allowing designers to become more and more creative with their work. Bikes are getting lighter, more durable, and better performing."

Specialized Bicycles offers these tips for the aspiring bicycle designer:

1. A bachelor's of science, particularly in an engineering field, certainly helps. Industrial design is another area of study that can be of great value.

2. Many bike companies, Specialized included, like to see applicants who have some experience working in bicycle retail, or at least a connection to the outdoor sporting goods world.

3. Barnett's Bicycle Institute (www.bbinstitute.com) and United Bicycle Institute, UBI, (www.bikeschool.com) are great resources for all kinds of bike building skills. UBI has classes that focus specifically on frame building in a variety of methods and materials.

4. Ride your bike. Think about what can be done to help a bike perform better or improvements that will lead to people enjoying the sport more.

When considering developing your skills to become a bicycle engineer, consult the want ads or manufacturer's Web sites to see what types of jobs are being offered and focus your development efforts on the skills needed by employers in the industry.

Do you know how to use AutoCAD or Pro-E (Pro/ENGINEER) design software? Having a good knowledge of the capabilities of the software packages is a good way to get started. Expose yourself to as much of the industry as possible. Read every bicycle book, magazine, and article you can find. Making friends with your local librarian will go a long way toward obtaining almost any book or magazine that you want on bicycles. Most libraries will order books for you, if they don't have it on the shelf. Become as much of an expert as possible. Participate in the forums at many of the manufacturer's Web sites. Follow McLaughlin's advice and get started. The more you know about the bicycle industry, the better your chances of gainful employment right out of college.

> **Employment Ad for Bike Engineer**
>
> The requirements for this visible position are a BA/BS in engineering and a minimum of two years' experience in design/development and manufacture of bicycles; working knowledge of AutoCAD and Pro-E design software a plus. Travel and vendor interface experience a must. Proven successful experience in taking ideas from prototype to finished product.
>
> The Specialized Bicycles Web site (www.specialized.com)

Engineers who do this:

- **Manufacturing Engineers**—Determine systems to get bike-related equipment manufactured. Interested in reducing the costs associated with production.
- **Materials Engineers**—Always on the lookout for new materials to have more fun, increase performance, and provide a more comfortable ride. This includes anything that makes up the bike such as the frame, forks, hubs, tires, grips, and seats or bike gear such as clothing, helmets, and shoes.

- **Mechanical Engineers**—May design the frames, derailleur, hubs, forks, handlebars, brakes, spindles, sprockets, and everything in between.

Bicycle-related companies that hire engineers:
- Campagnolo—www.campagnolo.com
- Cannondale—www.cannondale.com
- Easton Sports—www.eastonsports.com
- K2 Sports—www.k2sports.com
- Performance Bicycle—www.performancebike.com
- Shimano—www.shimano.com
- Specialized—www.specialized.com
- SRAM—www.sram.com
- Terry Bicycles—www.terrybikes.com
- Trek—www.trekbikes.com

More resources:
- Adventure Cycling Association—www.adventurecycling.org
- AutoCAD—www.autodesk.com
- Bicycling Magazine—www.bicycling.com
- Bike World—www.bikeworld.com
- How Mountain Bikes Work—www.howstuffworks.com
- International Sports Engineering Association—www.sports-engineering.co.uk
- Pro/ENGINEER Software—www.ptc.com
- The Bicycle and the Engineer—www.princeton.edu
- USA Cycling—www.usacycling.org

SWIMMING

Tom Westenburg, Principal Engineer,
United States Olympic Committee

"I became involved in sports engineering in a roundabout way. I was always interested in sports growing up, but didn't realize that I could make a career out of it. I was a distance runner in college, did low-level racing in sailing, and skied. Growing up, I liked to figure out how things worked. I was good at math and science and became interested in music, stereos, and sound processing. I was interested in many different fields of study, but electronics was the area that really grabbed my attention.

"My father was an engineer at Lawrence Livermore Lab but never really talked about where he worked. One time he managed to get approval to take me on a tour of the facility. I couldn't believe there was so much cool equipment! It was fascinating and mind-boggling. From that point on, I was hooked; I had to go into engineering.

"My first job as an electrical engineer was with Phillips Corporation in Holland working on integrated circuit designs. I was lucky and able to work in an area that did instrumentation and some interesting music and audio applications, such as Dolby™ noise reduction and some of the early work in digital audio and voice synthesis. My main focus was to convert analog signals into digital values for real-time processing or storage. At this point, I had no idea that this same technology would lead me into space applications and, eventually, into sports engineering. For example, instrumentation is needed to monitor the speed of your car, the position of the space shuttle, or the impact force of a boxer's punch.

"I had been through the Olympic Training Center on a tour and thought it would be the ideal job to work developing state-of-the-art equipment to enhance athletes' performance. Years later, I came through Colorado on a ski trip and noticed the engineering position in the newspaper. I applied immediately and have been with the U.S.

Olympic Committee ever since. I design various electronic devices to measure athletic performance. These are custom sports-specific systems that aren't commercially available. The instrumentation can look at impact forces, monitor position, or whatever the sport needs to try to help an athlete improve. It's a lot of data acquisition, sensor, and embedded controller design. One thing that I love is that it's always

changing, and I never know what my next project will involve.

"A few years ago, we did a project for swimming that was very successful. The idea came from a coach who thought that if a swimmer could learn what it felt like to swim faster, with assistance, then, when the assistance was removed, the athlete would be able to progress quicker. We started looking at this and came up with basically a miniature ski lift over the pool. It had a cable about nine feet above the water that attached to a tether and a harness around the athlete's waist. It used steel cable and needed about 4,000 pounds of tension in it. This required wall anchors, guy wires, guide pulleys, etc. At that point, I'm glad we took a step back and realized that the high tension was really just to keep the weight of the cable from sagging. We changed to a small Vectran cable (10 times the strength of steel by weight) and only needed about 300 pounds of tension, which allowed us to do away with almost all of the extraneous hardware. This new version was very simple and not nearly as impressive looking as the indoor ski lift would have been, but it allowed us to just mount the system into standard pool starting block holes.

"The next issue was how to drive the cable to tow the athlete. Having a high-power electric motor on a pool deck didn't seem very safe. So we went with a hydraulic motor. Then, we moved the drive motor and a hydraulic pump down to the pool pump area. This kept the noise, as well as the high voltage, away from the athletes and coaches. Then we looked at types of hydraulic fluid, in case a line broke and fluid was spilled into the pool with athletes in it. Some types are fairly  toxic, so we went with a fluid about like vegetable oil. Unfortunately, this went rancid after a few months, since anything could grow in it. Later, we went with a very safe but just slightly toxic fluid. A person needs to drink over a liter before it would cause problems, so if an athlete drank some from a film in the pool, it would be totally safe.

"Everybody in the first group to use this system set personal records at their first competition, and two set world records. This was after only six weeks of training, so we felt like the system did work and the concept was solid. In my position at the U.S. Olympic Committee, I get to work with some of the best athletes in the world and get to experience many sports that I never knew existed until I took this job. Many times the designers are also the "test pilots," so we get to try out a new instrumented boxing bag, take a luge sled down a start ramp, or paddle our instrumented kayak. Like I said before, I never know what to expect next, but I wouldn't want it any other way."

Swimming Equipment Design Today

You may be wondering how engineering can enhance swimming, but perhaps a better question would be what couldn't engineering do for swimming? To enhance the sport of swimming, engineers design everything from the swimming pool that reduces turbulence generated by the swimmers to the swimsuit that reduces the swimmer's resistance through the water, to the high-tech computerized racing systems used at Olympic events.

To help swimmers swim faster, scientists and engineers decided to study fish. Engineers at MIT built a robotic fish to study its movements. Researchers at other institutions are creating other models to study strokes to better understand where the power comes from. Engineers and scientists at Adidas found that the following variables enhanced a swimmer's performance:

> *"Studying engineering lent a sense of discipline to my athletics. Engineering requires organization, and that taught me how to budget time for studies, extra curricular activities, practice, and meets."*
>
> **Lisa Ackerman,
> Civil Engineer**

1. Body temperature—Studies indicate that athletes have more power when they run a slight fever. The higher temperature induces chemical reactions that make muscles contract faster.

2. Drag—When swimming, water sticks to your body and forms a boundary layer called surface drag. However, researchers found that this didn't happen to the Mako shark. The shark was able to move quickly through the water because of a V-pattern in its skin. The bodysuits that were developed with this pattern had less resistance than human skin.

3. Muscle oscillation—This is a problem in many sports that causes fatigue. Muscle oscillation is when an athlete's muscles in motion look like Jell-O®. Bodysuits help reduce oscillation because they aid in compressing the muscle.

4. Tight suits—Wearing a tight suit enhances a swimmer's performance through what is called proprioception. Proprioception refers to the nervous system's interpretation of its body position based on how the suit presses against the skin. Athletes who feel stronger and more in tune with their muscles will perform better. According to Adidas, "The suit creates compression that allows the nervous system to provide

better feedback on where the body is positioned."

Aside from suits, there is tremendous engineering that goes into designing a swimming pool for Olympic competitions. The governing body for Olympic swimming pool design is La Fédération Internationale de Natation Amateur (FINA). FINA specifies the depth, width, length,

space between the lanes, and temperature of the pool. Engineers who designed the solar heating system at the aquatic center that was used during the 1996 summer Olympic games worked tirelessly to determine how to maintain 1,000,000 gallons of water at 78 degrees Fahrenheit.

In the 1920s, Olympic hopefuls vied for the gold medal by swimming in cold, dark water. Today, swimming pool engineers enable swimmers to swim faster in a cleaner, temperature- regulated, and generally more pleasant environment. However, a major problem in racing is surface turbulence. Each swimmer in a lane creates wave patterns that have the potential of increasing the turbulence for other swimmers. Engineers determined that the best way to decrease turbulence was to move the swimmer's wakes to the bottom of the pool. If the waves were allowed to move from side to side, they would only create more waves. By using pumps to increase the surface tension or pressure on the surface of the water, engineers were able to reduce wave action. One hundred and one inlets arranged in a 360-degree pattern, as well as extra gutters, allowed swimmers from 24 countries to break more than 120 records during the 2000 Olympic games!

There is no limit to the number of things that engineers can do to enhance swimming. Other technology in swimming that is quickly coming to the forefront includes using computer simulations to analyze and optimize strokes. By careful analysis, scientists and engineers have been able to gain solid evidence about how the body actually moves through the water, and it may soon be possible to determine the perfect stroke. Miniature computer displays indicating lap time, timers, and the current time are being mounted inside goggles or on swim gear to provide information to the swimmer while swimming. Fins are being designed with new tough and flexible materials to help divers kick easier and transfer more power with less effort.

Engineers who do this:

- **Biomedical Engineers**—May design new suits or model a swimmer's performance on computer systems to analyze stroke capabilities.
- **Chemical and Materials Engineers**—May develop fins, suits, performance training equipment, and new diving boards that allow more or less elasticity while maintaining their strength and durability.
- **Civil Engineers**—May design swimming pools that reduce waves for competitions or design heating systems that keep the pool at a constant temperature.
- **Electrical Engineers**—May develop better timing and computer systems to keep track of the athletes.
- **Mechanical Engineers**—May design swimming treadmills or other mechanical systems that increase swimming performance.

Swimming-related companies that hire engineers:
- Colorado Time Systems—www.coloradotime.com
- Daktronics—www.daktronics.com
- Speedo—www.speedo.com

More resources:
- International Sports Engineering Association—
  www.sports-engineering.co.uk
- La Fédération Internationale de Natation Amateur (FINA)—
  www.fina.org
- USA Diving—www.usdiving.org
- USA Swimming—www.usswim.org

PARATHLETES

Jay Humphries,
Mechanical Engineer and Tester, Seattle Systems

"...So how do you get a job like this?" asks a young man, unaware of Humphries' background. "Well...," Humphries hesitates, "first, you lose both of your legs."

Upon first appearance, Humphries looks, walks, and acts just like any other 32-year-old. If you ask him what he thinks about his handicap or if he considers himself a hero, he'll deny those labels. Because that's the kind of guy he is. Yet, spend a day in his shoes and you'll come to realize that he deserves to be outspoken, perhaps even a bit arrogant, if for no other reason than to inspire hope. Try to keep up with him during a typical workday and you're in for a humbling experience. He is driven like the wind. He walks with a slight limp, but it doesn't slow him down. The first real indication that you might get about his differences comes when he shows up for a weekend mountain bike ride in shorts, then it hits you like a face plant on the hard-packed clay trails that have become Humphries' weekend stomping ground. Yeah, he's just an ordinary, 32-year-old guy with one, slight exception—he's missing both his legs. Wait a minute...that's why there's a limp.

In 1991, Humphries and four other airborne soldiers were dropped off onto a hilltop near the town of Dahouk, Iraq. It was standard operating procedure to deploy small teams tasked with scouting an area prior to U.S. troop advancement. Unfortunately, on this particular mission, Humphries didn't walk out.

He enlisted in the Army when he was just 18 years old and graduated from both basic training and airborne school in Fort Benning, Georgia. He was then assigned to the 3rd Battalion, 325th Airborne, stationed in Vicenza, Italy. After about a year as a rifleman, he was assigned to the battalion's reconnaissance platoon. Immediately after the Desert Storm cease-fire in 1991, Humphries' unit was sent to northern Iraq to help protect the Kurdish people from Iraqi aggression.

"We were there in Iraq for about two weeks, when my battalion started pushing toward the town of Dahouk," he recalled. "My reconnaissance team, which had five members, was dropped off by helicopter onto a mountainous ridge."

After making their way to a hilltop that overlooked a crossroad, the five soldiers set up an observation post in an old defensive position that others had built by piling up loose rocks. There was barbed wire, and land mines were everywhere. Humphries speculated that either the Iraqis or the Kurds could have built the defense, and there may had been fighting there in the past, based on the many shell casings that were scattered about.

On May 4, 1991, the fourth day of the mission, Humphries and two other soldiers set out to patrol the area. "We noticed more mines on the way out of our position that morning, but we didn't let it get to us," Humphries said. Later, as he was leading the way back to the observation post, Humphries stepped on a buried land mine. The explosion severely damaged both of his legs, which had to be amputated above the right knee and below the left knee. He had suffered intestinal damage, a dislocated elbow, a perforated eardrum, and, worst of all, the explosion also robbed Humphries of sight in both eyes. But, after months of rehabilitation and surgery, he regained sight in his right eye, which has a corrected vision of 20/20 with glasses.

Humphries misses the adventure and the sense of camaraderie that military life once offered him. But, recognizing that he still has contributions to make to the world, he earned his bachelor's degree in mechanical engineering from The Johns Hopkins University in Baltimore, Maryland. "I was so beaten up by the land mine incident, that once I had healed up physically and got sight in my right eye back, I realized the only thing holding me back was the current state of the art in the prosthetic industry," he explained. "So I pursued my education in engineering."

Humphries began working for United States Manufacturing, a manufacturer of orthopedic and prosthetic products in January 2001 as an engineer and product tester. He moved to work in the Poulsbo, Washington, plant in 2004. He currently wears the new Seattle Systems high-performance foot, called the Cadence HP, which has been recently introduced into the market. "Under my circumstances, after all I've learned from my life—from school and from working at Seattle Systems—I am glad to be able to help develop more advanced prosthetics," he said.

When he is not at work, Humphries can be found pedaling up Green Mountain or the trails near Port Gamble on his mountain bike, which he does three or four times each week. "Covering a lot of distance under my own power, over difficult terrain is something that was really missing from my life. The mountain bikes that are available today offer just about anyone the ability to ride difficult terrain with a greater degree of comfort than ever before. Not to mention that it is just incredibly fun and a great way to get exercise."

On weekends, he skydives out of Kapowsin, Washington, usually getting in seven jumps a weekend, weather permitting. According to Humphries, jumping from military planes is nothing like the sport jumping that he does today. He has made over 2,500 sport skydives. "I only jumped static line when I was in the Army. The goal was to get a lot of guys on the ground as fast as possible, usually at night, and loaded with equipment and weapons. It was thrilling, but not nearly as fun as sport jumping, where I am in free fall for about a minute, and I have a parachute that lands me softly," he explained. More experienced skydivers like Humphries often downsize their parachutes to increase their landing speed, which happens at more of a horizontal glide than at a vertical drop. That means most skydivers have to land at a run. For Humphries, with two prosthetic feet, landing is easier when he uses an inline skate wheel device (that he made) that fastens to his prosthetic knee. "When I land, I plane out my parachute just above the ground. I am still moving with significant velocity, too fast to run. I start to drag my right toe along the ground, so the knee flexes. Then I settle down onto that wheel like I am taking a knee, rolling out the rest of the way. It worked great on the hard ground in California," he noted. Since Washington's soil is much softer, Humphries has learned that his landing wheel doesn't roll quite as efficiently, so he's mulling over ideas for new inventions. "I have to redesign the wheel," he said, "because, when I land here, the wheel tends to sink into the ground, and I have been known to face plant on occasion."

Parathlete Equipment Design Today

Every day, parathletes participate in snow skiing, golfing, mountain climbing, archery, Ping-Pong, tennis, biking, basketball, volleyball, rugby, bowling, horseback riding, skating, fishing, sailing, and more. In the hands of a creative engineer, there is no limit to what can be done to improve the life of a person with a disability. Amputees, spinal cord injury survivors, and paraplegics are getting around and having fun playing many different types of sports.

One of the most popular wheelchair sports today is basketball, with 181 teams in 22 conferences. The chairs are considered to be part of the player's body. The wheelchairs for each sport are usually custom-made to fit each athlete and the sport he is playing. The parathlete who plays a contact sport such as football, hockey, or rugby requires a much different chair than the athlete playing Ping-Pong or volleyball. In basketball, the chairs must be manual, but, in hockey, the chairs can be either manual or electric. In rugby, the chairs are sport-utility wheelchairs.

Athletics for people with disabilities really started in 1948 with the International Wheelchair Games. The games eventually grew to include many other sports and categorized the various disabilities. In 1988, the Paralympic games became standard fair, always following and in the same venues as the Olympics. The sports organizations that develop the selection criteria, select the athletes, foster development, and generally run the games are the United States Association of Blind Athletes (USABA), The United States Cerebral Palsy Athletic Association (USCPAA), Disabled Sports USA (DSUSA), The United States Wheelchair Athletic Association (WSUSA), and the Dwarf Athletic Association of America (DAAA).

The Paralympics differ from the Special Olympics in that the Special Olympics allow people with cognitive impairments to compete, where Paralympics involve athletes with physical impairments. All people who meet the criteria can enter, and all the competitors win medals and prizes.

As wheelchair sports evolve, so does the equipment. Would the sports evolve on their own, without the engineers, or do the engineers contribute such advancements to the equipment design that the sports

are allowed to evolve? There is a whole market now that produces wheelchairs for athletes. They are made to endure the most vicious attacks of aggressive sports and, at the same time, provide exceptional handling ability for the participant.

Designers usually have to give sport wheelchairs a low center of gravity, to make the chair more stable. The seat angle, frame length, over-all height, backrest, and seat adjustability are other equally important characteristics of sport wheelchairs. The angle that the wheel makes with the ground is called the wheel camber, and the correct angle adds tremen-dously to the chair's stability. With a higher camber, the chair can be hit repeatedly without falling over. The higher camber also allows for more maneuverability and less drag. Lightweight wheelchairs cut down on shoulder and wrist injuries. Many manufacturers now use titanium tubes, because they are twice as strong as aluminum and half the weight of steel. Using titanium for the rims is also beneficial, because titanium lessens the heat from the player's hands by absorbing and dispersing it.

Racing wheelchairs are different from other sport wheelchairs, because of their unifork crown system. They have brakes like a regular bicycle and look like a sporty, high-tech recumbent three-wheel bike. Among the rac-ing wheelchairs are handcycles. The formation of the U.S. Handcycling Federation (USHF) prompted handcycling to become an officially sanc-tioned competitive sport in 1998. Handcycles now exist for every type of athlete, from the rigorous competitor to the recreational rider and kids. You can see handcyclists admiring the ocean from a beach path as well as view-ing the sunset from a weaving mountain road.

Jeremy Adelson, an engineer with Seattle Systems, spoke about the difficulty associated with designing custom equipment for athletes. "When I am designing a custom brace, there is no flat surface on the human body or leg from which to work," he explained. All bodies are unique, and no two projects will ever be identical.

To increase the performance level of some athletes, Next Step Orthotics and Prosthetics developed a custom-fit, microprocessor-con-trolled hydraulic knee. Now, above-knee amputees can walk without a limp, and athletes can run without the jarring effects associated with regu-lar prostheses. The prosthetic knee is a piston-and-oil system that mimics the natural movements of the knee.

Another challenge faced by engineers in this industry is the lack of information available. Designing a mono-ski or other sports equipment for skiers or athletes requires continuous study and extreme patience. Athletes who are paralyzed below the waist cannot always tell the engineer the entire performance story, because they cannot feel what the equipment is doing all the time. It's a challenge unique to this industry. To supplement the feedback systems, video analysis, time testing, wind tunnel testing, and empirical testing are all necessary.

The National Sports Center for the Disabled offers summer and winter internships for students interested in working on assistive technology projects for athletes.

Engineers who do this:

- **Biomedical Engineers**—May design new equipment to aid in mobility and research the motion of many sports to determine the requirements for a specific sport.
- **Chemical and Materials Engineers**—May develop or design new lightweight materials that will be more comfortable and withstand greater impacts or forces.
- **Computer/Software Engineers**—May design software or hardware to aid in pressure or impact detection analysis, manufacturing processes, or information systems.
- **Mechanical Engineers**—May design systems for manufacturing or testing new products or be involved in building and testing prototypes.

Parathlete-related companies that hire engineers:

- Altimate Medical—www.easystand.com
- Johnson and Johnson—www.jandj.com
- New Halls Wheels—www.newhalls.com
- Seattle Systems—www.seattlesystems.com
- TiSport—www.tilite.com

More Resources

- American Wheelchair Bowling Association (AWBA)—www.awba.org
- International Paralympics Committee—www.paralympics.org
- National Wheelchair Basketball Association—www.nwba.org
- Palaestra Magazine—www.palaestra.com
- Sports 'n Spokes Magazine—www.sns-magazine.com
- The National Sports Center for the Disabled—www.nscd.org
- U.S. Handcycling Federation—www.ushf.org
- U.S. Quad Rugby Association —www.quadrugby.com
- Wheelchair Hockey League (WCHL)—www.wchl-michigan.com
- Wheelchair Tennis—www.itfwheelchairtennis.com

Chapter 3

Sports Support Careers

HELMETS

Dennis K. Lieu,
Professor of Mechanical Engineering,
University of California at Berkeley

"When I was in school, I never had much interest in sports. I had neither the time nor talent for it. I was born in the United States, but my parents were immigrants from China. Since neither of them had the opportunity to attend college, they viewed a higher education as the key for a successful life. They constantly reinforced this philosophy throughout my school years. I attended school at UC Berkeley because it was close to home, it was affordable, and I could get in. My interest in engineering didn't develop until I was a freshman there. I took a basic physics class, because all my friends were taking it, too. It was then that I discovered that I not only enjoyed the material but also was fairly good at it. While searching for a career that would allow me to apply physics, I met Professor C. Dan Mote, who introduced me to the world of engineering. He would later become my graduate study advisor, lifetime mentor, and good friend.

"Mote was an avid skier, and part of his research work involved the application of mechanics to improve ski-binding design. This work was absolutely fascinating to me. Even though I was not a skier, I found that the operation of ski-bindings could be explained mathematically. More important, by understanding the mechanics of how ski-bindings functioned, they could be improved. This was a case of engineering applied to biological systems. I eventually continued to study the topic of safety equipment design in graduate school and received my D. Eng. degree in mechanical engineering at UC Berkeley.

"After I completed school, I found that I had a bit of spare time on my hands. I decided to study martial arts for reasons of health, discipline, and culture. I trained regularly and rigorously, eventually earning a 4th degree black belt in Taekwondo. Since sparring competition was a large part of my training, I watched and participated in many tournaments. In Olympic-style tae kwon do sparring, full power kicks are permitted to the head and torso. Padded headgear and chest guards protected these areas of the body. I recalled many tournaments where competitors required medical attention and were even taken to the hospital in ambulances, after receiving a particularly hard or well-placed blow. Out of concern for the safety of the competitors, as well as for myself because I was also involved in competition, I decided to investigate how the headgear and chest protectors were designed and tested to ensure that they adequately protected the wearers.

"The results of my investigation were surprising. In many sports such as football, hockey, and cycling, there were industry standard tests and specifications that had been developed to ensure that the helmets used functioned to some minimum performance levels. Yet in martial arts, with repeated hard contact to the head and torso, no such standards existed. Many different equipment styles would appear at tournaments, with some designs obviously better than others. Equipment design was largely by trial-and-error. Competitors would sometimes use the thinnest and lightest gear they could find, believing that it would give them an advantage in mobility, without regard to safety.

"I found, once again, that I had the opportunity use my engineering skills to improve sports safety, this time in a sport that I understood and loved. As with ski-bindings, protecting the head and torso from injury was a matter of understanding the mechanics of the body and the devices used to protect it. It was all a matter of engineering. The injury process could be explained mathematically. As a professor at UC Berkeley, I had the academic freedom to pursue research into protecting the head and torso from impact in contact sports, and I pursued this opportunity. After developing accurate mechanical models to simulate the human head and torso and an accurate method of striking these models with a simulated kick, a simple equipment evaluation test was produced. This test was composed of a swinging aluminum arm that would strike a simulated head wearing headgear or a simulated torso wearing a chest guard, at a predetermined speed. The acceleration of the simulated head or internal pressure inside the simulated torso, would need to be below a prescribed minimum level, in order for its protector to be considered a good piece of equipment. This simple test could be used to quickly evaluate new safety equipment designs and eliminate unsafe designs from being used in the field, thus making the sport safer for its participants."

Helmet Design Today

Biking, skateboarding, football, hockey, race car driving, baseball, inline skating, motorcycle riding, snowboarding, skiing, martial arts, and many more sports all have two things in common: helmets and the engineers that design them! Without helmets, athletes in many sports could suffer skull fractures, severe concussions, and internal bleeding that could lead to brain damage, paralysis, or even death. Helmets reduce the severity of injuries by providing cushioning that protects the head by absorbing or dispersing the impact

energy over a wider area, thereby lessening the potential for neck and spine injuries.

When two beefy, 300 lb football players run full speed at each other (seven yards per second) from 18 feet apart, the collision produces enough energy to toast a piece of bread or light a 100-watt light bulb for more than three seconds. From all the power produced by collisions in one football game, you could probably power a tiny city all day. With all that power happening on the field, helmet designers have created airbag helmets that inflate when subjected to at least 500 pounds of force. Another design appears to reduce the G-forces of some hits by 30%.

The Insurance Institute for Highway Safety reported that 98% of bicyclists killed in 1999 were not wearing helmets. Wearing a helmet during a crash reduces the risk of head injury by 85%. Newer helmets not only look cool but also are aerodynamic and lightweight, provide ventilation, and evaporate sweat on hot days and wick away moisture.

A fascinating application of biomechanical engineering, according to Ellen Morrissey and Donald Lehr of the Nolan/Lehr Group, involves helmets for hockey players. Although the helmets appear to be made of a single piece of material, they are actually three different parts fitted together in an intricate geometric configuration for maximum energy absorption. To test the helmet's ability to withstand and dissipate impacts, manufacturers fit helmets with instrumental test heads and then drop them several meters. At the end of the drop, known as a "sudden deceleration," the testers examine the helmet's level of protection and whether it has withstood impacts of 300 Gs or 300 times the force of gravity (your body weight). An example will help to illustrate how the helmet must perform. The force of the impact of a bicycle rider colliding at 30 mph into a concrete wall is the equivalent of 80 Gs. If the cyclist weighs 100 pounds, the impact will feel like 8,000 pounds pressing on the cyclist's head, which shows how critical that helmet is to the cyclist's survival! The engineers in this industry function like the behind-the-scenes rescue squad. They save lives every day by preventing injuries before they happen.

Besides providing protection, helmets must be designed properly to be light and keep the head cool, because most athletes who need head protection are in constant motion and release a great deal of heat through their head. Heavy helmets can increase neck strain and impair movement. Lightness allows players to accelerate at high speeds and then, because sudden stops square the effect of inertia, stop without tumbling off balance.

The three parts of a NASCAR helmet include the outer shell, the BeadALL liner, and the inner liner that is made of the padding and fastening hardware. NASCAR also must make helmets fire retardant so that they don't melt or combust. The outer shell consists of glass, Kevlar, carbon, and other materials that make it very hard and give it a glossy appearance. The visor that is attached to the helmet and works as a windshield is made of a plastic material similar to bullet-proof glass.

The BeadALL liner provides a second level of defense against impacts. It is made of more energy-absorbing material such as polystyrene or polypropylene. Newer helmets have a one-piece BeadAll liner design for better comfort and fit.

The inner liner includes fire-retardant materials, cheek pads, and chin straps. This layer is flexible and form-fitted to the driver's head. Because of varying head shapes, two heads that are the same size (even when measured with a tape) will not fit the same helmet. If the helmet does not fit properly, it will not adequately protect against impacts.

Helmets are further tested for optimal design in wind tunnel experiments. The helmet must reduce drag, offer good protection against wind forces, and not lift or pull up on the driver's head. Excess drag, lift, and side-to-side motion can cause neck strain and impair a driver's vision.

Engineers who do this:

- **Biomedical Engineers**—May design systems to analyze the human body wearing the helmet for neck and spine injury prevention and research the motion of many sports to determine the requirements for helmet design.
- **Chemical and Materials Engineers**—May develop or design new lightweight materials that will be more comfortable and withstand greater impacts or forces.
- **Computer/Software Engineers**—May design software or hardware to aid in pressure or impact detection analysis, manufacturing processes, or information systems.
- **Industrial Engineers**—May maintain bills of materials and routings information, determine cost standards, and recommend pricing for

new products, as well as be involved in learning about and training others in manufacturing techniques.

- **Manufacturing Engineers**—May design systems or processes for
manufacturing helmets more efficiently.
- **Mechanical Engineers**—May design systems for manufacturing,
motion analysis, or impact testing and may be involved in building
and testing prototypes.

Helmet-related companies that hire engineers:
- Bell Sports—www.bellsports.com
- Bieffe Helmets—www.matrixsports.com
- DuPont—www.dupont.com
- ProTec—www.pro-tec.net
- Riddell—www.riddell.com
- Simpson Race Products—www.simpson.com
- Trek USA—www.trekbikes.com

More resources:
- Airflow Sciences—www.airflowsciences.com
- American Society for Testing & Materials—www.astm.org
- Head Protection Research Laboratory—www.hprl.org
- Helmet Manufacturer's Directory—www.smf.org
- Southern Impact Research Center—www.soimpact.com
- Sporting Goods Manufacturing Association—www.sgma.org

SHOES

Jennifer Ocif,
Performance Footwear Engineer, Reebok International, Ltd.

In 1993, with an undergraduate degree in mechanical engineering from Rensselaer Polytechnic Institute, Ocif began working at a medical device manufacturer in the research and development department. She worked with biomedical engineers who had interesting stories about their course work and piqued her interest to go to graduate school. She wanted to study something that would become the foundation of a new, people-oriented, and human-applied career that would be interesting, challenging, and fun.

She had always been an athlete and was curious to apply engineering principles to the human body in motion. That's when she decided she wanted to work as an engineer in the sporting goods industry.

In 1995, while working towards a master's degree in biomedical engineering at the University of Iowa (UI), Ocif heard about a design contest from a fellow graduate student, Michelle Sabick, sponsored by the

Sport Science and Technology Division of the United States Olympic Committee (USOC) in Colorado Springs, Colorado. It sounded so cool to design something that would help U.S. Olympic athletes win gold medals. The 1996 summer Olympic games were coming to Atlanta the following year, so the national Olympic spirit was in high gear. Despite her heavy graduate school workload, she and her friend Sabick entered the contest. It was the contest of a lifetime, because, as engineers studying biomechanics, they were the perfect contestants. If anything, Ocif knew she would have fun tinkering with a homemade science project to see what she could come up to help U.S. athletes.

They consulted with the late Dr. Jim Hay, their advisor at UI and one of the top sport biomechanists in the world who studied track and field. Based on his research, they developed an inexpensive motion-tracking device to pinpoint the location of an athlete's footfalls on the track during training or competition. Dr. Hay's research had shown that foot placement, especially during the approach of a triple jump or long jump, directly affects an athlete's performance. At the time, Dr. Hay's research with track and field athletes depended on an expensive video motion analysis system that required several months of data analysis after the day of filming. Frustrated and anxious athletes and their coaches needed faster performance feedback. Dr. Hay challenged Ocif and Sabick to build a small, lightweight, inexpensive, real-time data acquisition and analysis motion tracking system that high school, college, and Olympic coaches could use to help train their athletes. Dr. Hay wanted to enable the coach to see an athlete's foot placement relative to the take-off board even before the athlete got up from the sand pit after completing the triple jump or long jump.

> *"Pursue what you love, figure out if you can turn it into a career and a rewarding job, and make things happen for yourself. Don't simply let things happen to you, by taking the path of least resistance…. Make them happen for a reason, to achieve your goals. Make sure you can look forward to going to work every day. If you love what you do, you'll have fun at it, your strengths and achievements will naturally emerge, and you and your teammates will succeed! Both on and off the playing field!"*
>
> **Jennifer Ocif,**
> **Performance Footwear**
> **Engineer, Reebok International, Ltd.**

Ocif and Sabick investigated possible solutions and submitted a design proposal to the USOC judges, who had been working with Olympic athletes for years. A few months later, they received a letter that their design had been chosen as one of five finalists out of more than 20 applications! Excitedly, they began to build a prototype using ultrasonic transmitters, ultrasonic receivers, parts bought at Radio Shack, plastic orange cones, and wires. They used their electrical engineering textbooks to design the circuitry and consulted an electrical engineer to help build the circuit boards. Ocif and Sabick's device resembled a car key-chain remote control, in both weight and size. They tested the assembled prototype by attaching it to the laces

of their own sneakers and running at the university track. It took about six months to a year to develop and $500 to build the first working prototype—after learning from a few failures. As with Thomas Edison, those early failures were key to their success!

In 1996, they traveled to the U.S. Olympic Training Center in Colorado Springs with Dr. Hay to present their final design and prototype to the USOC judges. The competition was tough, but the judges awarded them a first place prize of $1,000, a trophy, and an exclusive tour of the sports biomechanics labs, where they saw several Olympic athletes in training. From this point on, Ocif knew that she would combine sports and engineering into a fun and intellectually and monetarily rewarding career. She hopes one day to help U.S. Olympic and Paralympic athletes win gold medals.

At Reebok, Ocif designs, engineers, develops, and evaluates athletic footwear with a team of coworkers in the U.S. and in Far East countries, with the goal of marketing and selling performance-driven footwear worldwide to athletes young and old, male and female, recreational and competitive.

Shoe Design Today

Running, biking, climbing, hiking, skateboarding, speed skating, rollerblading, bowling, and playing basketball, football, soccer, tennis, volleyball, and many more sports, all have two things in common: Shoes and the engineers who design them! Almost every sport has specific shoe requirements, and engineers must analyze the movements and cushioning needs of the athletes to determine the best shoe possible for reducing injuries, enabling outstanding performance, feeling comfortable, and looking great.

The Olympic contenders of the early 1900s had shoes made of leather that probably weighed two or three pounds. The Olympic contenders of today wear shoes that weigh only two or three ounces. Beyond making shoes lighter, though, shoe designers must accommodate the requirements of the specific sports. A skateboarder wants a shoe with a sticky sole to grip the board and provide more traction. A bicycle rider wants a shoe with a rigid sole to transfer more power to the pedal. A basketball player wants a shoe with ankle support and a sole that grips well while running but not while turning or pivoting. A runner wants a shoe with good cushioning that won't break down quickly. A marathon runner wants a shoe with built-in microchips to provide data on timing and position. According to Dolores Thompson, a process engineer at Nike, "It has been helpful to have a familiarity of sports, fitness, and teamwork. Specifically, to understand the different performance needs of cushioning. Cleated foot-wear (soccer, football, softball) has different cushioning performance needs than court (tennis, basketball) or even running or rock climbing." To assess cushioning needs, designers have used everything from air pumps to silicon to other synthetics, in an attempt to increase the fun and comfort of athletes everywhere.

Athletes frequently sustain injuries to their knees and Achilles tendons. In the Nike Sports Research Lab, scientists and researchers study the motion of athletes in many different sports to design shoes that will help to minimize the risk of injury. To design a safe shoe that helps soccer players make swifter kicks, a high-speed video camera captures

The most important skills an engineer needs before applying for jobs in the sports engineering field are:

1. Hands-on human subject research and/or project work in electro-mechanical, material testing, sports biomechanics, manufacturing, or CAD engineering (depending on the specific engineering position and sports application).

2. Scientific design of experiments with human subjects.

3. Technical writing and excellent communication skills. Fluency in another language is helpful.

4. Anatomy, kinesiology, and physiology classes.

5. Literature review skills: Being able to quickly research a topic through journal articles.

6. Statistics: Testing products can require extensive data collection.

video data of a player kicking the soccer ball at 1,000 frames per second. To design basketball shoes, researchers identify many different foot movements of players, analyze the motion with high- speed motion analyzers, measure the forces applied to the ground, and record the pressure from sensors inside the shoe. Each and every movement must be recorded and analyzed to provide the greatest flexibility and performance potential to the athlete. These types of data help the designers understand the dynamics of the sport, where the most pressure is applied during movement, and the needs of the athlete, in order to anticipate the requirements of the athletic shoe. Final prototypes are then made and may be tested again.

In addition to using engineers to apply biomechanics to shoe design and perform research such as motion analysis, shoe companies hire industrial, manufacturing, and mechanical engineers to ensure that shoe manufacturing processes go smoothly. Materials have to arrive on time, inventory has to be controlled, and the manufacturing processes have to work according to specification. Dan Barch, an industrial engineer for Nike explained, "The entire 'supply chain' needs to connect, like an organism—for real success. It all has to work together. Nike uses a lot of sport analogies, and this could be like basketball or soccer—you have your position and function but can see everyone else and where the ball is. Sometimes you shoot, sometimes pass off quickly, and sometimes hold. It depends on the situation and everybody's position. Any professional acting independently of the rest of the team—or team acting independently of the company—quickly finds themselves benched for the big plays."

Chemical and materials engineers will also find a wealth of employment in the shoe industry. Constantly on the lookout for new materials for soles and outer coverings, shoe manufacturers compete to provide the best cushioning, lightest overall design, and most comfortable and best traction products. Finding new materials that add breathability for the long distance runner, springiness for basketball players, increased traction for skateboarders, flexibility and grip for wrestlers, more cushioning for long jumpers, and strength and comfort for skeleton racers can make the shoe industry a challenging and rewarding field for an athletically minded engineer.

Engineers who do this:

- **Biomedical Engineers**—May study motions and forces occurring with the human body during sports movement to evaluate a product, in order to enhance performance and reduce injuries.
- **Chemical, Materials, and Textile Engineers**—May develop or design new soles, fabrics, or other materials for shoes.
- **Computer/Software Engineers**—May design software or hardware to aid in pressure or impact detection analysis, manufacturing processes, or information systems.
- **Industrial Engineers**—May maintain data on the materials used, their price, and cost standards and recommend pricing for new products, as well as be involved in learning about and training others in manufacturing techniques.
- **Manufacturing Engineers**—May design systems or processes for manufacturing shoes more efficiently.
- **Mechanical Engineers**—May design systems for manufacturing, motion analysis, or impact testing or be involved in building and testing prototypes.

Shoe-related companies that hire engineers:

- Adidas—www.adidas.com
- American Sporting Goods Corporation [Avia, Apex, Nevados, Ryka, Turntec, Yukon]—www.americansportinggoods.com
- ASICS—www.asicstiger.com
- Converse—www.converse.com
- Nike—www.nike.com
- Reebok—www.reebok.com
- Saucony—www.saucony.com
- Sketchers—www.sketchers.com
- Timberland—www.timberland.com

More resources:

- Athletic Footwear Association—www.afa.org
- Engineer a Sneaker Activity Guide—www.wepan.org
- Sporting Goods Manufacturing Association—www.sgma.org

BROADCAST ENGINEERING

**Cindy Hutter,
Vice President and General Manager,
Fox Sports Net, Houston Technical Operations Center**

"The Houston Operations Center is a 100,000-square-foot, white, metal building in an industrial neighborhood, just outside the famous Galleria area in Houston. You wouldn't know much happened in here from the outside. Inside is one of the largest technical television program playback centers in the country.

"What we do at the Houston Tech Ops Center:

- Take in tapes from program suppliers for the purpose of broadcasting them on Fox's regional sports networks.
- Receive live professional and college sporting events, via either fiber optic line or satellite, to broadcast them on the regional sport networks.
- Add commercials and graphics to the live and taped shows.
- Digitally compress 14 program streams into five satellite transponders, to permit their broadcast to some 8,000 receivers at cable company "head-ends" all across the country.

"The Houston Tech Ops Center has 23 fully digital master control rooms, all run by an automated system. At any given hour, one operator controls three networks at a time. Most recorded programs are played to air off one of 10 video servers, with a total storage capacity of 15 terabytes.

"Outside the facility are the technicians who work in the "live trucks" at the ball fields to produce and transmit the games back to Houston. It is these technicians who have to know the most about sports to be able to work in the business. The rest of our broadcast engineering work is rather universal—it's the same across sports, news, commercial production, and entertainment.

"My primary responsibility is to oversee the entire process of the Technical Center—300 employees in eight departments, ranging from graphics to the video library. It is my job to find ways to make the broadcast process more streamlined, both from a technology and manpower perspective. I have degrees in electronics and journalism with a focus on radio and television operations. Many large-market television stations like to hire directors of engineering with an electrical engineering degree.

"I definitely had a lucky break. I graduated from college in the mid-1970s, when female technicians and engineers were difficult to find, and TV stations were hiring all of them that they could. In 1979, I got a "summer vacation temporary engineer" position at ABC News (and spent the summer in the electronic maintenance shop fixing TV monitors and soldering multi-pin connectors on camera cables). I was able to stay at ABC for a number of years, working in all the technical areas, gaining a lot of experience, which included exciting engineering assignments in locations like Brazil, the Himalayas, and all over the world. This background made it possible for me to later attain senior engineering management positions (including several stints as director or VP of engineering) for several television stations around the country. From that background, I was able to attain my present position at the network.

"As you can see, it is extremely important to find an entry-level job, such as my paid summer temp job (a lot of TV stations and other TV companies hire extra technical help in the summertime so that the regular engineers can take vacations) or an internship at a television facility, in order to "get your foot in the door." Real-world experience makes all the physics and math come alive, and you gain an understanding of how video, audio, and data move around a television facility and the principles behind video flow—something that is very difficult to teach in a classroom. Another possibility is to work at a local cable access channel—many won't pay much, but it's invaluable experience.

"I was lucky enough to know what I wanted as a career soon after I started working at the student radio station in high school, when I was 15. I've worked in radio, concert mixdown, and, since graduating college, television broadcast engineering."

Media in Sports Today

Computer analysis in sports today is a booming business. Computer engineers not only work to get the broadcasts out to your TV or the Internet but also are responsible for the yellow first-down line on the screen during football games, for immediately knowing the distance a baseball was hit, for showing football plays or speed skating maneuvers by drawing on your television screen, for knowing how fast the horses are running at the Kentucky derby, for timing ski championships anywhere in the world, for creating the virtual strike zone on ESPN Sunday

Night Baseball, for coordinating the instant replays for Monday Night Football, and much more. Any technology that enhances your entertainment benefit is something that engineers work to achieve.

Roberto Peon, a senior software engineer for Sportvision, Inc., a company that creates broadcast enhancements for the sports broadcast industry, was a student at Georgia Tech when Sportvision came to recruit. "I started out doing computational perception in the graphics visualization and usability lab at Georgia Tech and then began doing

special effects in a new class taught by my advisor. One of the guys from Sportvision came to our school to give a talk about the yellow line (i.e., a real-time TV special effect) for the DVFX (Digital Video Special Effects) class, which I had taken the previous term. I talked to the Sportvision guy after the talk and he hired me."

Painting the virtual yellow-line is a monumental task. According to HowStuffWorks.com, a number of problems have to be solved before the system can even begin to work:

- The system has to know the orientation of the field with respect to several cameras, so that it can paint the first-down line with the correct perspective from each camera's point of view.
- The system has to know exactly where every yard line is, and it has to be able to sense when players, referees, or the ball cross over the

first-down line, so it does not paint the line right on top of them.
- Given that the cameraperson can move the camera, the system has to be able to sense the camera's movement (tilt, pan, zoom, focus) and understand the perspective change that results from the movement.
- Given that the camera can pan while viewing the field, the system has to be able to recalculate the perspective at a rate of 30 frames per second as the camera moves.
- A football field is not flat—it crests very gently in the middle to help rainwater run off. So the line calculated by the system has to appropriately follow the curve of the field.
- The system also has to be aware of superimposed graphics such as logos and athlete biographies, that the network might overlay on the scene.

Engineers are also hard at work on the instant replay system for televised football games. Leitch Technology has developed a system that allows officials to quickly review a play. When instant replay first came out in the early 1980s, it was on videotape and took a large amount of time to review. The players and the fans would become frustrated, so the instant replay was banned from football in 1991. With digital recording, there are no tapes to rewind or fast-forward, and officials can review a play immediately. In fact, the rules dictate that they only have 90 seconds to review the play and make a decision.

If the world of broadcast engineering fascinates you, there are many things that you can do to prepare for this adventure. Peon of Sportsvision says that, for engineering students interested in applying for jobs in sport engineering, "a hands-on, can-do approach is by far the most important trait to have. Technical knowledge about computer graphics, algorithms, and geometry (vectors and matrices) are also important, but if you are intelligent and motivated, these things will come naturally."

Engineers who do this:
- **Computer/Software Engineers**—Write programs for the "Sports Ticker"—a program that blends sports wire data with a graphics package. (You see tickers on a number of networks, both news and sports—MSNBC, CNN, Fox News, ESPN, and Fox Sports Net.)

- **Electronic Maintenance Engineers**—Repair and maintain the equipment.
- **Information Technology Engineers**—Build and maintain the WAN (wide area network) and the national "Video-over-ATM" network.
- **Operations Technicians**—Run the master control rooms and operate the equipment to put the programming on the air.
- **RF (Radio Frequency) Engineers and Technicians**—Keep the satellite uplink and downlink equipment functioning properly.
- **Technical Design Engineers**—Design and build the electronic systems in the operations center.

Broadcasting-related companies that hire engineers:

- ABC—www.abc.com
- ESPN—www.espn.com
- FOX Networks—www.fox.com
- Sportvision—www.sportvision.com

More resources:

- Broadcast Engineering Magazine—www.broadcastengineering.com
- HowStuffWorks—www.howstuffworks.com
- The Society of Broadcast Engineers—www.sbe.org

FOOD FOR ATHLETES

Betsy Willis,
Food Processing Engineer, Southern Methodist University

"The car was filled with anticipation of a great mother-daughter bonding experience...a trip to the mall. The conversation turned to sales. Not just which stores were having sales, but how to determine the sale price of an item based on its original price and the percentage discount. During that short ride to the mall, my younger sister and I, then ages four and eight, learned a practical, yet important, math lesson—the relationship between fractions and percents.

"Such was life in my house as a child...math and science everywhere. What would appear to be a simple question about math homework turned into a lesson on engineering, thanks to my father (an engineer). Science fair projects were encouraged and supported, and excellence in math and science were expected. My father worked as an engineer for a petroleum company and occasionally brought home some plastics that he made in the lab. But I did not fully understand what he did as an 'engineer.' However, my parents set me on a path to success by expecting outstanding academics while remaining active in a variety of other activities.

"Throughout my high school years, I was enrolled in AP math and science, as well as English and history. I took tap, jazz, and ballet lessons; performed with a dance company; and served as captain of the school dance team. I was also involved in various school clubs. Throughout my life, the answer to the question "What do you want to be when you grow up" ranged from professional ballerina to elementary school teacher to physician. Uncertain of exactly what I wanted to do in life, I started college at Purdue University as a chemistry major.

"Arriving at Purdue as an excited, nervous freshman, I embarked upon my college studies. About a month into the fall semester, I attended the Industrial Roundtable, a large job fair with 200-plus companies represented. I talked with various companies, mainly consumer products companies, about the job opportunities. In these conversations, I learned that I really wanted to make things...and that is what engineers do! So, I talked with one of the freshmen engineering advisors, who listened to my interests and suggested food process engineering. That day, I even met a food process engineer, who created the macaroni and cheese shaped like dinosaurs—she explained to me how engineers used math and science to "engineer" the shape of the pasta such that it does not fall apart during boiling! I also learned that food process engineers deal with the mass production of foods, beverages, and pharmaceuticals—sounds easy enough, but not when dealing with the inherent variability of nature. While I had never heard of food process engineering before, I thought it sounded interesting and like a field with good job security—we will always have to eat!

"During my undergraduate engineering studies, I co-oped with Kellogg's and had the opportunity to work in various departments within the company. While at Kellogg's, I realized that the engineers with graduate degrees were assigned the more challenging and interesting projects—the kind of projects I would like to work on someday. Thus, I decided to pursue graduate studies at Purdue in a fast-track program to a PhD. Over the next five years, I was on the forefront of scientific discovery, as I developed and validated a mathematical model for moisture transport within foods. Although I am not employed by a food company using my degree directly, I do have the opportunity to share my engineering experience with others by relating math, science, and engineering to food.

"I credit my parents for setting the standards high, expecting excellence in math and science, and encouraging me to remain balanced. They enabled me to stand at my high school graduation and make the choice to do anything I wished in life. Had they not pushed me to excel in math and science, completing calculus and four years of science in high school, I would not have had the opportunity to become an engineer."

Power Food Design Today by Betsy Willis

What is the most efficient way to rehydrate a team during a timeout? What nutrients should be included in a fitness bar for top performance? How can marathoners refuel without missing a step?

Food process engineers address these questions and more every day. Food process engineers create foods and beverages in mass quantities and lead product development, process development, and production troubleshooting. Realizing that athletes have special nutritional needs, food process engineers also work with specialists to create foods and beverages to provide the human body with the nutrients needed for top performance.

So, are food process engineers like chefs? Food scientists? Nutritionists? Food process engineers borrow and learn from these other occupations, while actually applying engineering concepts to food.

Food process engineering (FPE) is a specialization within the fields of agricultural and biological engineering and chemical engineering. FPE applies concepts from traditional fields of engineering, like mechanical and chemical engineering, to biological products. Sounds easy enough, but consider that Mother Nature never makes anything exactly the same twice and consider the complexity of the human body. Biological and agricultural products vary from season to season, field to field, plant to plant, and even grain to grain. Consider, too, all of the complex processes that the human body conducts to convert foods and beverages you consume into usable energy. Food process engineers overcome these challenges by using biology, chemistry, food science, math, and engineering and by working with a team of experts in a variety of fields.

Creating foods and beverages requires a team approach from engineers to nutritionists to scientists to businessmen. Each person contributes individual talents and knowledge to the creation of new foods and beverages. Food process engineers must consider how math and science affect the texture, flavor, appearance, and smell of foods and beverages. For example, what geometric shape (math) and what ingredients (science) should be used to make an energy bar that will not crumble with the first bite?

In developing new food and beverage products, food process engineers and their team follow four basic steps:

1. Identify the need, target consumer, and possible solutions.
2. Formulate and test possible solutions. (This requires processing and tasting.)
3. Refine the recipe, process, and packaging. (This requires more processing and tasting.)
4. Get the new product to the marketplace fast!

Consider sports beverages with annual sales of more than $1 billion. How do you make enough to supply the entire U.S., let alone the whole world? Engineers, scientists, nutritionists, and business-people tackle challenges just like this every day in the food and beverage industries.

How would you make a sports beverage?

The Challenge:
To formulate a food or beverage to rehydrate and replace lost electrolytes.

The Criteria:
- Easy to consume
- Provides water
- Provides electrolytes
- Provides energy
- Easy for the body to absorb
- Tastes good
- Easy to transport

The Need:
During exercise, an athlete loses water and electrolytes through sweat, which if not replaced, leads to decreased performance and, in extreme cases, death.

The Solution:
To create a food/beverage to meet all the criteria and the challenge.

The advantages of FPE:
- Challenging, due to the variability of nature
- Uses knowledge in a variety of subject areas including math, science, food science, and engineering
- Benefits society by creating delicious, fun, nutritious foods and beverages

- Good job security—people will always have to eat!
- Fun—what other job pays you to eat and play with food?

Engineers who do this:

- **Chemical, Agricultural, and Biological Engineers**—May design food for athletes that provides more nutrition, more protein, or more energy or research ways to make food last longer or be more convenient.
- **Mechanical and Manufacturing Engineers**—May design food packaging systems or manufacturing processes.

Food process-related companies that hire engineers:

- Accelerade—www.accelerade.com
- Camelbak—www.camelbak.com
- Clif Bar—www.clifbar.com
- Gatorade—www.gatorade.com
- G-push—www.gpush.com

More resources:

- The Institute of Food Technologists—www.ift.org
- The Principles of Sports Nutrition—www.gpush.com
- The Science of Hydration—www.gatorade.com
- UC Davis Food Science and Technology— http://foodscience.ucdavis.edu

Chapter 4

Sporting Facilities

STADIUMS, ARENAS, TRACKS, AND COURSES

Jeff Bresee, P.E.,
Civil Engineer, Enprotec and Hibbs & Todd (EHT)

"I am a hydraulics specialist. I specialize in the design, specification, and installation of granular infill synthetic (GIS) Turf fields. I have explored various methods of turf manufacturing and have worked with the turf industry to optimize the manufacturing design of GIS Turf.

"Engineering has been the perfect ticket for me to make the world a better place. I didn't know I wanted to be an engineer until my sophomore year in college. I was always very artistic, had a good eye for color, as well as mathematically inclined. I wanted to pursue a career that would let me be creative and artistic. I wanted to be outdoors and use my math skills. Civil engineering seemed like a good fit, because it was a hands-on career working in the field.

"I got into the sports turf business by being in the right place at the right time.

Players were suffering knee and head injuries from playing on 'green cement' or artificial turf. Schools were spending $1 million on playing surfaces that were being destroyed in three years. I saw the opportunity and, now, the players are much better off.

"I have extensive knowledge of drainage and geotextile materials. I work with manufacturers to create products that will maximize the cost efficiency of field drainage. I also worked with the rubber industry to create an infill gradation that will optimize field performance (speed and agility) while, at the same time, maintain a safe G-Max rating (hardness guidelines for synthetic/infill systems set by the U.S. Consumer Product Safety Commission).

"The end result is a not just a GIS Turf field, but a premium GIS Turf field at a cost that is, in many cases, less than that of fields that have been installed in the past. I also have expertise in the design, specification, and installation of other athletic venues, such as synthetic tracks, softball fields, and baseball fields."

Stadium Design Today

Stadium, arena, and course design is such a broad topic, it could be a book in itself. The many aspects of designing these large venues for sports events are some of the most challenging, intriguing, and comprehensive projects for engineers. The most common degree for this aspect of design is civil engineering, but many projects also call for mechanical, environmental, electrical, computer, materials, and chemical engineering.

Stadiums are built to stand the test of time. There are so many different technologies at work in stadium and sports event design that almost any type of engineer can be involved. The Toronto Skydome, built in 1989, was the first stadium to have a retractable roof, and it only opened over a small area in the center. The Houston Astros stadium, now called Minute Maid Field, built only 11 years later, was an amazing engineering accomplishment, in that it has the largest open area of any retractable roof. The idea of retractable roofs was to have a stadium that could be indoor or outdoor and allow the playing field to have natural grass instead of artificial turf. Artificial turf was causing many injuries to athletes and ended a few careers too early.

The roof of the Astros stadium is composed of three panels that cover 1,263,240 square feet of stadium. The north and south panels are 528 feet by 125 feet and weigh approximately 1,905 metric tons. The middle panel is even bigger; it is 589 by

242 feet and weighs 3,810 metric tons. If you do the math, you will find that the roof has a total weight of 15,240,000 pounds. It rolls out on the tracks on 140 steel wheels with their own braking mechanisms that are 36 inches high. The roof has the ability to open up on nice days or close under adverse weather conditions such as high humidity or rain. With such a large distance to travel, the roof takes 12–20 minutes to open completely.

Built by HOK Sports Facilities Group, the stadium cost $250 million and was awarded the Most Outstanding Civil Engineering project by the Texas section of the American Society for Civil Engineers.

But stadiums are not just about the roof. Lighting, acoustics, air conditioning, seating, emergency procedures, safety issues, big screens for playbacks, computer controls, and the playing surface all come into play. Every aspect of the design requires trained engineers to make it function and perform as expected. When we attend a ball game, we often don't even notice when everything works as expected. The engineering is invisible. But, if the engineering wasn't invisible, the players would miss catches, because the lighting produced glares; we would be uncomfortable in our seats; the sound system would blare at inappropriate times, or we may not be able to hear it at other times; the air-conditioning may not keep us cool; and the turf on the stadium floor would injure the players. The fun and engaging sports we came to see would be no fun at all, as the players limped home and we waited for their injuries to heal.

The playing fields are usually made of grass, artificial turf, or synthetic systems. Artificial turf or Astroturf came about because of the need for a grasslike playing field for the Astrodome, the world's first air-conditioned stadium. The idea for an indoor stadium was remarkable, except that the glare produced by the dome windows or skylights made it impossible for the outfielders to see and catch the balls. To reduce the unwanted glare, the skylights were painted a dark color, and, without sunshine, the grass died.

AstroTurf was just like real grass except that it was synthetic, hard, and worsened with age. It was made of one-half inch to one-inch nylon fibers interwoven into a mat that was laid on concrete, rubber, or crushed stone. Players were sore from falling on it, and it contributed to many injuries such as knee twisting, tendonitis, shin splints, torn Achilles tendons, and many different types of sprains. The only good things about AstroTurf was that it was very durable and didn't need water to stay green all year.

The new synthetic/infill grasses available today are a combination of grass and artificial turf and go by the names of FieldTurf, AstroPlay, and SprinTurf. These new systems are two inches to two-and-one-half inches of grasslike fibers, interwoven into a polyethelene backing, and then filled with rubber or silicon pellets. It is much easier on the players and has reduced the injuries that were prevalent on artificial turf surfaces. To make sure that the surface is doing a good job, the U.S. Consumer Product Safety Commission has created hardness guidelines called G-Max ratings. Now, hard, injury-producing fields are not even allowed on the market.

Another innovative design advance for the playing field comes from engineers at Rehau, Inc. The Cleveland Browns stadium in Ohio is subject to excessive frigid temperatures and cold winds. Every winter, the snow and ice would freeze the football field, injure players, and kill the grass. Engineers assessed the situation and installed 40 miles of pipe on gravel under a sandy soil mixture. The right amount of heat from the underground heating system keeps the grass growing longer and keeps the field from freezing.

Arena Design Today

Skating rinks for the Olympic games are another amazing feat of engineering. To the casual observer, an ice rink is an ice rink, right? Wrong! Engineers strive, through a painstaking process and marvel of engineering, to create the fastest ice possible. Faster ice can mean new world records.

The temperature of the ice, the humidity, the height of the ceiling, and all the air in between is strictly controlled. Even the air purity is strictly maintained. How do engineers do it? Thirty-three miles of one-and-one-half inch pipe that transport 1,000 tons of chilled saltwater below the ice is one challenge. Saltwater is used, because it can be kept in liquid

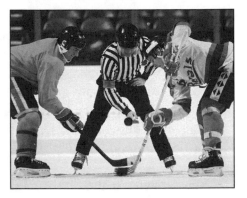

form at a lower temperature than regular water. The pipes of saltwater are set four inches apart and form a network under the entire arena.

Another part of the process enables engineers always to know the exact temperature of everything in the arena. To measure the temperature of the ice, 12 thermometers measure the actual ice, eight thermometers measure the temperature of the air above the ice, and another four infrared thermometers are set in the ceiling to detect changes in the surface. These 24 thermometers transmit the temperature data to a computer that can send extra shots of cold saltwater to the exact spot in the ice that may be getting warmer or can turn up the air-conditioning in the arena.

What makes ice fast? Reducing the oxygen in the ice makes it harder and freeze faster. Because of this knowledge, engineers are able to create a skating rink that is only three-quarters of an inch thick (thinner than an ice cube), is superfast, and can stand up to constant pounding.

Skating rink ice is comprised of 25–30 layers of ice set on top of concrete. Deionized or ultrafiltered water (water that has been stripped of as many impurities as possible) is sprayed onto the rink and allowed to freeze before another layer is sprayed. This process is repeated until the ice reaches the desired thickness. The temperature is lowered for freezing the first few very thin layers, so that they freeze very fast. When these layers are frozen, the ice is then painted white to reduce the glare and to give it the appearance we are used to. The paint is then sealed with several more layers until it reaches one-eighth of an inch in thickness. After the sealing stage, another 20 or so layers of ice are set on top, and the formation is completed.

Creating a rink in high altitudes can give engineers an advantage in creating fast ice. Higher altitude means that there is less oxygen in the air. With less oxygen in the air, less air freezes in the ice layers. Dehumidifiers that can reduce the oxygen in the air to just 3% are also used while creating the ice and during the games, to keep the ice drier.

Another consideration in creating superfast ice is dust. Dust particles must be eliminated to keep the ice pure. In the Olympic games, air-purifiers are constantly at work, so that as little dust as possible lands on the ice.

Now, imagine that 6,000-7,000 jumping and screaming fans have entered the arena to support their country. Engineers must determine how much power the air-conditioner must have to produce enough cold air to keep up with the heat generated from all the people.

Speed skaters in long races, such as the 3,000-meter, 5,000-meter, and up, like the ice very hard. They use long strokes to glide at speeds of 40-plus mph. Fast ice is their friend. Skaters in shorter events such as the 500-meter like the ice a bit softer, so that their skates can grip the ice and allow them to dig in for more speed. By a feat of engineering, rinks are now built so that the computer-controlled temperature can be adjusted from race to race, to allow the athletes to achieve peak performance...or break world records.

Track Design Today

Running tracks need to accommodate the athlete and event. Running long distances is hard on the human body. The constant impact of foot to pavement can make your feet, knees, and back hurt. A softer running surface for this sport is essential. The surface is actually made to absorb the impact by distributing the energy at the impact point to a larger area. The running surface for sprinters tends to be springier to give them lift and speed.

Running tracks don't apply to just humans but are for horses, too. Racetracks are made with advanced technology, to prevent injury to the horses and extend their running careers. These tracks usually have a six-inch sub-base, a nine-inch base, and a three-inch cushion. The first step in creating a track is to assess the weather and location of the track. Samples of the rock formations and underground water sources are also critical.

The construction must begin during fair weather. Each layer of the base must be done to specification. Wet soil will shrink when it dries, and dry soil is dusty and won't compress properly. Tracks built in rainy or cold weather climates require limestone bases, because limestone drains well. Tracks in drier climates require clay, because it holds some moisture to form a better running surface. The choice of materials is extremely important, because the wrong materials can lead to horses breaking their legs, cannon bones, or knees.

The track drainage system is important, to prevent the track from being washed out in a heavy rain. The track must drain evenly, or it can become unsafe for the horses. For a safe track, the horses must

be able to run in the rain or just afterwards without slipping, and they must also not damage the track with the combination of pounding and water. Just like tracks for Olympic contenders, the horses also need tracks that provide cushion and bounce.

Racetracks require maintenance, and a well-maintained track will last longer. Changes in temperature change the track from day to day. Rolling the track and keeping it watered in hot weather will keep it soft and the horses and riders happy.

Engineers who do this:

- **Chemical and Materials Engineers**—May work to develop or design new materials that enhance the participant or spectators' enjoyment.
- **Civil Engineers**—May design stadiums, arenas, or other sports event facilities or any system in a sports event facility.
- **Computer/Software Engineers**—May design software or hardware to regulate arena temperature or design computers or networks to control information systems.
- **Electrical Engineers**—May work with the high-speed cameras to improve the clarity of images taken at the finish line.
- **Mechanical Engineers**—May design any system in a sports event facility.
- **Structural Engineers**—May design stadiums, arenas, or other sports event facilities.

Sports facility-related companies that hire engineers:

- Alpha MRC, Inc.—www.alphamrc.com
- Barton Malow—www.bmco.com
- Clough, Harbour & Associates LLP—www.cha-llp.com
- DuPont—www.dupont.com
- Ellerbe Becket—www.ellerbebecket.com
- HNTB—www.hntb.com
- HOK Sports Facilities Group—www.hoksports.com
- L. Robert Kimball & Associates—www.lrkimball.com
- Lamp, Rynearson & Associates, Inc.—www.lra-inc.com
- OLYMPVS INTERNATIONAL AG—www.olympvs.com
- Wood & Zapata—wood-zapata.com

More resources:

- National Council of Acoustical Consultants—www.ncac.com
- American Society for Civil Engineers—www.asce.org
- American Society for Mechanical Engineers—www.asme.org

Chapter 5

Getting Started

Remember that this book is only one source of information to help you decide whether you want to become an engineer. Right now, you need to begin reading everything you can find about engineering and talk to every engineer or engineering student you know about the challenges ahead and how to prepare for them. Attend a summer camp or program pertaining to engineering at your school. Obtaining this information now may save you lots of heartache if you decide later that you are on the wrong path.

Academic preparation is also essential to exploring engineering as a career. In addition, getting involved in extracurricular activities pertaining to engineering can give you invaluable exposure. In high school, classes in algebra I and II, trigonometry, biology, physics, calculus, chemistry, computer programming, or computer applications can tell you if you have the aptitude and determination to study engineering. All of the above courses are not required to get into every engineering school, but early preparation can mean the difference between spending four years in college or six. Some universities also require two to three classes in a foreign language for admission. Check into the programs that interest you, and begin to fulfill their requirements. Advance Placement or Honors courses and an ACT score of 20 or SAT of 1000 are recommended.

Junior Engineering Technical Society (JETS)

JETS is a national society dedicated to providing students with guidance and information about engineering. The Society offers many programs that will help you decide if engineering is the career for you. Students, teachers, and parents also gain exposure to the social, political, and economic impact that engineering can have on our lives.

JETS offers activities, events, competitions, programs, and materials to educate students about engineering. Examples of competitions and programs include:

- Tests of Engineering Aptitude, Mathematics, and Science (TEAMS). TEAMS is a national academic competition that enables groups of high school students to learn team development and problem-solving skills. Students learn how math and science concepts are applied to real-world problems. Teamwork is promoted in an open-book, open-discussion environment, and students often have an engineering mentor.

  In the past, competition problems have included real-world challenges such as bridge design and rehabilitation, flood analysis, food preservation, solar-powered vehicle design, and air transportation. The wide range of real-world problems shows students the diversity of specialties within the engineering field.

- National Engineering Design Challenge (NEDC). NEDC is a competition that challenges high school students to design, fabricate, and demonstrate a working solution to a real-world need.

- National Engineering Aptitude Search+ (NEAS+). NEAS+ helps individual students determine their level of basic engineering skills. Students can determine if additional math, science, or reasoning skills should be acquired.

- Uninitiates Introduction to Engineering (UNITE). In cooperation with the U.S. Army, JETS offers UNITE, a summer initiative for minority students who want to pursue their interest in engineering and technology study and build their math and science knowledge and skills.

If JETS interests you, check out their Web site at www.jets.org. The site is packed with additional information about the different careers in engineering, programs offered, competitions, activities, and events. JETS is an excellent source of information for you as you continue to explore the many aspects of engineering as a career.

Summer Camps

Summer camps provide another innovative approach to preparing for a career in engineering or evaluating if that career is right for you. Find out what it is like to study engineering and learn about the different types of engineers and what engineers do on a daily basis. Almost every college of engineering offers a residential or commuter summer engineering camp for high school students. The camps offer students a week or two of fun, while developing leadership, professional, and personal organizational skills. The camps also provide opportunities to meet and talk with engineers during visits to local engineering companies. Check with the college of engineering at a university near you to see if any summer programs are offered, or visit the Engineering Education Service Center's Web site at www.engineeringedu.com to find a camp in your area.

Student Competitions

A great way to get a feel for engineering is to participate in the student design competitions that are sponsored or cosponsored by various engineering societies and organizations. These competitions are developed to encourage and motivate students. The competitions focus on teamwork and allow the students to get a "real-world" feeling of the design process, cost of materials, and team dynamics and environment.

A few of the more popular competitions include:

- Boosting Engineering, Science, and Technology (BEST). A robotic competition that provides students with an intense, hands-on, real engineering and problem-solving experience that is also fun. (www.bestinc.org)
- FIRST Robotics Competition. Corporations and universities team up with high schools in a high-tech robot sporting event. (www.usfirst.org)
- Mathcounts. A national math coaching and competition program for 7th and 8th grade students. (www.mathcounts.org)
- Future City. Students learn about math and science in a challenging and interesting way throuogh reality-based education using SimCity 2000 software. (www.futurecity.org)
- TEAMS and NEDC. (sponsored by JETS; www.jets.org)

- International Bridge Building Contest. The construction and testing of model bridges promotes the study and application of fundamental principles physics and also helps high school students develop "hands-on" skills through bridge construction. By participating in the Bridge Building Competition, students get a flavor of what it is to be an engineer, by designing structures to a set of specifications and then seeing the structures perform their function. Students are also provided with an academically oriented extracurricular activity that is recognized school-wide. (www.iit.edu)
- Odyssey of the Mind. A worldwide program that promotes creative, team-based problem solving for students from kindergarten through college. (www.odysseyofthemind.com)
- National Science Bowl. A U.S. Department of Energy academic competition in which teams of high school students answer questions on scientific topics in astronomy, biology, chemistry, mathematics, physics, earth, computer, and general science. (www.scied.science.doe.gov/nsb)
- BattleBots IQ. BattleBots IQ is a comprehensive educational program in which students learn about the science of engineering through robot building. This unique curriculum fuses mathematics, physics, and engineering into tangible and relevant lessons for high school students. (www.battlebotsiq.com)

For a more comprehensive list of competitions, visit the Engineering Education Service Center's Web site at www.engineeringedu.com.

Undergraduate Engineering Competitions

Many competitions are also sponsored by the student chapters of many engineering societies. These competitions are often very complex and are among teams of engineering students competing nationally against engineering students at other universities. The projects often require excellent communication and coordination within the teams, and strict deadlines must be adhered to. The prizes range from trophies to cash and scholarships.

Examples of contests include Helicopter Design, Tractor Pulls, Future Car, Human Powered Vehicle, Concrete Canoe, Robotics Automation, Radio-Controlled Aircraft Design, Solar Powered Vehicle Design, Steel Bridge Building, Submarine Races, and more.

Contact your engineering department to find out what contests are available at your school.

What Now?

Now that you have decided to pursue an engineering education, you should prepare for it as soon as possible. Search the Internet and contact any societies that are of interest to you. Browse their Web pages. Ask about their programs to help you prepare for college. Ask to talk to students currently participating in programs that interest you. Contact local engineering firms, and ask for a tour. Most firms would be happy to show you around and explain what they do. Several companies encourage continuous improvement in engineering and science education. For example, a company may have a summer intern program that allows college-level science students to work at the company's facility each year. Companies also may sponsor a shadow-the-scientist program to bring junior high and high school students into the facilities or labs to see what the researchers are doing.

If you like the companies you're in touch with, ask if they offer summer internships or job shadowing programs. Through this simple effort, you will make a contact, and, more important, a potential job opportunity may await you when you finish your degree.

Choosing the Right School

Choosing the engineering school that is right for you is as important as wheels are to automobiles. Your choice will incorporate many of your preferences. Making the selection won't be easy. Hundreds of schools offer engineering programs. The advantages and disadvantages of each school will depend on your personal needs and wants. Important considerations for most college-bound students include location, cost, faculty, school size, and academics.

- Location: In addition to distance from home, location refers to climate and the type of industry in the surrounding area. If there is industry specific to your degree, then opportunities for summer internships, co-op programs, and part-time work experience increase dramatically. These work experiences often lead to jobs after graduation.

- Cost: Cost of attendance may be a critical factor in determining which school to select, although your decision should not be based on cost alone. Generally, public institutions are less expensive than private schools, but there are numerous ways to fund education at any institution. Most engineering societies offer scholarships, and the government offers grants and loans. Part-time work, co-op programs, and campus jobs also help reduce the cost of attendance. Check with the financial aid department of the schools you are interested in to see what grants and loans you qualify for. Call the engineering department to find out about scholarships offered to incoming students through the college. The military may also offer opportunities for financing your education. The National Guard is a popular program among college students. The Air Force, Coast Guard, Marines, Merchant Marines, Army, and Navy offer education at reduced cost in exchange for a commitment to serve in the Armed Forces for a certain period of time.

- Faculty: A fine faculty makes it easier to get a good education. A faculty that includes women and minorities will broaden your experience and better prepare you to work with people from diverse backgrounds. Faculty members can bring a variety of experiences and expertise to their lectures. Check to make sure that faculty rather than graduate students teach the classes. As you proceed to your junior-level and senior-level classes, the research of the faculty becomes more important. Try to select a school that has at least one faculty member performing active research in your area of interest. That person can be a role model. You can learn directly from someone whose interests you share.

- School Size: School size matters for some students. Large schools offer a greater diversity of people and more things to do, but often lack the professor-student interaction found at smaller schools. In a small school, you may get to know a larger percentage of classmates, but in a large school you can meet a much greater number of people. You can receive an excellent education at a large school or a small one; which you choose is purely a matter of preference.

- Academics: Academics is probably the most important factor in choosing the school that's best for you. The program should be accredited by the Accreditation Board for Engineering and

Technology (ABET). ABET accreditation ensures that the school program follows national standards for faculty, curricula, students, administration, facilities, and institutional commitment. By choosing an ABET program, you can be sure that the faculty has met certain national standards and that the program is highly regarded by the profession. Some students like the competitive atmosphere that accompanies attending a very prestigious school, and some students find they work better in a more relaxed environment. Both will require a great deal of studying, although some programs will be more challenging than others. Pick the atmosphere that best fits your personality and aspirations. Questions you might ask at this point include: Do I want to be on the cutting edge of technology? Do I want to find better solutions to existing, identifiable problems, even if a current solution already exists? Or do I want a combination of the two?

- Some schools require their students to have computers; other schools provide computer laboratories. Find out if free tutoring is offered through the school and if the professors have posted office hours. Can you e-mail questions to professors? Will your questions be answered in a timely fashion? Another consideration is the campus library. Is it easy to find the information you are looking for? Does the school have a special engineering library or carry engineering journals?

Students frequently enjoy joining student chapters of professional organizations. These organizations can be an excellent resource during your college experience and in your career search. Many offer competitions against other colleges. Check to see if the society for the branch of engineering you want to study has student chapters at the schools you are considering. For details about student chapters and their activities, browse their Web sites.

Other school selection criteria to consider include sports facilities, leisure activities, community events, cultural events, and campus activity resources.

The Successful Student

Engineering is a rigorous and demanding major. To be successful in engineering school, you will need certain tools. You must be self-disciplined and manage your time effectively. In college, the "real" learning often takes place outside the classroom, and less time is spent in the classroom. A general rule of thumb says that for every hour spent in the classroom, engineering students can expect to spend three hours outside the classroom, compared with two hours for nontechnical majors. A good time-management system can also allow you to participate in extracurricular activities, which broaden your experience and are of interest to potential employers.

Engineering curricula vary from school to school, however, most schools don't require you to declare a specific field of interest until the end of your second year. The first two years of engineering school are focused on learning the fundamentals such as chemistry, calculus, physics, and mechanics such as statics and dynamics. Courses in English, the humanities, and biology are usually required as well.

The third and fourth years of engineering school are most often spent studying your chosen specialty. Most universities require their students to complete a design project in their senior year. The project may be completed in teams or individually and solves a real-world problem. Students may be able to select a problem of personal interest, or local industry may present a problem it is currently exploring. Typically, the project requires a research report and presentation of the design process and the results.

Co-ops and Internships

Cooperative education or a co-op experience is one where an engineering student alternates work experience in government, industry, or business with academics. For example, a student may do a parallel co-op where she works part-time and goes to school part-time, or complete a traditional co-op where she works for six months and goes to school for six months. A good co-op program may be the perfect answer for a nontraditional student who has financial responsibilities.

Because a co-op program is longer, the experience you obtain can be more meaningful. Additionally, a co-op experience can show employers you have a solid desire to work in your chosen field. In today's competitive market, you need to do everything possible to make sure you are the shining star.

Engineering internships are another way to get your foot in the door. They generally consist of a summer job related to your major at an engineering company. Many engineers began their successful careers by interning every summer. By the time they graduated, they were the first choice when a position became available. If you are interested in obtaining an internship position at an engineering firm, find a company you like and apply as early in the school year as possible.

What is a Professional Engineer?

A professional engineer (PE) is one who has been licensed by the state. Just as attorneys need to pass the bar exam and doctors need to pass the state medical board exam, engineers need to pass an eight-hour written exam called the Principles and Practice of Engineering.

Generally, to become a PE, you must graduate from an ABET accredited university, work for four years under the guidance of a professional engineer, and then pass the exam. Most states, however, offer a pre-registration certificate called the Engineer Intern to those who do not yet have four years of experience. You can obtain the Engineer Intern certificate by passing an eight-hour Fundamentals of Engineering (FE) test. The first half of the test challenges your general engineering skills. The last half pertains to a specific concentration in engineering such as chemical, civil, electrical, environmental, industrial, or mechanical. Although the certificate does not authorize the practice of engineering, it is the first step in the examination process for full licensure. Then, after you gain four years of experience, you can take the PE examination. This test relates specifically to a major branch of engineering.

Although licensure is not mandatory, there is a strong trend in the engineering community toward licensure. To be in private practice as a consulting engineer, for example, licensure is a legal requirement. Many high-level government positions can be filled only by professional engineers, and many states now require university instructors to be registered PEs. Most employers expect that students fresh out of college will be well versed in the basics or fundamentals of engineering. Engineer Intern certification proves them right. The National Society of Professional Engineers (NSPE) has information pertaining to the rules and requirements of licensure on their Web site at www.nspe.org.

Glossary

Alloy—the combination of two or more metals to optimize material properties. Most cast titanium clubheads, for example, consist of 90% titanium, 6% aluminum, and 4% vanadium, yielding a combination that is stronger than pure titanium.

Angler—person using pole or rod and reel to catch fish.

Balata—originally a derivative of the rubber tree, it once was used in the outer covers of all golf balls and makes an exceptionally soft-feeling golf ball. It was largely replaced in golf ball covers by Surlyn® and other man-made products. Balata is now produced artificially in laboratories, hence the difference between traditional balata (balls that would cut all the way through the cover) and modern balata (balls that dent more than they cut).

Bearings—consist of an inner and outer part, which the balls ride on, allowing the wheel to turn.

Blank—main component of a finished fishing rod, minus the guides and handle.

Carve—make a long, curving arc while skating.

Composite—a blend or mixture of different substances; the broad category of composite golf shafts includes graphite (graphite fibers mixed with resin) and other hybrid shafts not made entirely of metal.

Cooperative Education (Co-op)—a program that combines real-world experience with college classes.

Core—center of a golf ball, bowling ball, baseball, etc.

Coverstock—material that makes up the outer shell of a ball; the hardness, texture, and shine of a bowling ball.

Deck—also called a board; the platform that the hardware is mounted to, usually maple laminate.

Dimples—cup-like depressions on golf balls. Deeper dimples produce more spin, while shallower ones reduce spin and increase distance.

Durometer—an instrument for measuring the resiliency, or hardness, of a urethane wheel.

Fakie—riding backwards.

Fast Action Rod—a fishing pole that will flex initially in the upper one-third of its length.

G-Max rating—hardness guidelines for synthetic/infill systems, set by the U.S. Consumer Product Safety Commission.

Graphite—a lightweight substance employed in aerospace applications before its use in golf; graphite golf shafts are made with graphite fibers and glue (resin).

Grind—to ride on an object like a ledge or handrail with just the trucks making contact.

Iron Byron—the mechanical golfer unveiled in 1966 by True Temper, the world's largest shaft manufacturer, modeled after the swing of Byron Nelson. It was originally conceived to test shafts and now is used to test clubs, balls, and shafts.

Juiced—given extra energy.

Ollie—a no-handed air maneuver performed by tapping the tail of the board on the ground or ramp surface; named after Alan Gelfend.

Piezoelectric Device—an instrument that generates electricity to reduce vibrations in skis, bikes, snowboards, baseball bats, golf clubs, and more.

Prototype—original, full-scale, and usually working model of a new product or new version of an existing product.

Radius of Gyration (Rg)—identifies how fast a ball begins to rotate once it leaves the bowler's hand.

Reel Seat—mechanism that holds the reel to the rod, usually using locking metal rings or sliding bands.

Sealed Bearing—a bearing system that uses a physical seal to keep out water and debris.

Slow Action Rod—a fishing pole that will bend initially over its entire length.

Surlyn®—the most widely used cover substance for golf balls. The invention of this material led to the cut-proof golf ball. It is not as soft as balata, but unquestionably the king of indestructibility among golf balls.

Sweet Spot—precise point on a whacker where contact with the ball feels best.

Three-Piece Ball—ball that is generally manufactured with a solid or liquid center (first piece), surrounded by tightly woven rubber strands (second piece), and covered with a balata or man-made material on the outside (third piece).

Truck—hardware that is comprised of the axle and base plate mounted to the underside of the board.

Two-Piece Ball—consists of a solid core and a cover surrounding that core.

Wheel—rolling device that is usually made of urethane. In addition to the standard wheels, there are now those that have a nylon or high-tech plastic on the interior part of the wheel.

References:

- EXPN (X-Games)—www.expn.com
- PGA Tour and Golfweb—www.pgatour.com
- *The American Heritage® Dictionary of the English Language*, Fourth Edition—www.dictionary.com

Bibliography and Recommended Reading

Astin, Alexander. *What Matters in College? Four Critical Years Revisited*. San Francisco: Jossey-Bass, 1997.

Baine, Celeste. *Is There an Engineer Inside You? A Comprehensive Guide to Career Decisions in Engineering*. Eugene, OR: Bonamy Publishing, 2001.

———. *The Fantastical Engineer: A Thrillseeker's Guide to Careers in Theme Park Engineering*. Ruston, LA: Bonamy Publishing, 2000.

Bolles, Richard Nelson. *What Color Is Your Parachute? A Practical Manual for Job Hunters and Career Changers*. Berkeley: Ten Speed Press, 2001.

Brody, Howard, Rod Cross, and Crawford Lindsey. *The Physics and Technology of Tennis*. New York: Racquet Tech Publishing, 2004.

Byars, Mel. *50 Sports Wares: Innovations in Design and Materials*. Switzerland: Rotovision, 1999.

"Careers in Science and Engineering: A Student Guide to Grad School and Beyond." National Academy Press, 1996.

Congressional Commission on the Advancement of Women and Minorities in Science, Engineering and Technology Development. "Land of Plenty." Arlington, VA: Sept. 2000.

Davis, Susan, Sally Stephens, and The Exploratorium. "The Sporting Life: Discover the Unexpected Science Behind Your Favorite Sports and Games." New York: Harry Holt and Company, 1997.

Ferguson, Eugene S. *Engineering and the Mind's Eye*. Cambridge: MIT Press, 1997.

Ferrell, Tom. *Peterson's Job Opportunities for Engineering and Computer Science Majors*. United States: Thomson Learning, 1999.

Field, Sally. *Career Opportunities in the Sports Industry: A Comprehensive Guide to Exciting Careers Open to You in Sports*. New York: Checkmark Books, 1999.

Gabelman, Irving. "The New Engineer's Guide to Career Growth and Professional Awareness." New York: IEEE Press, 1996.

Haake, Steve. "Sports Engineering Journal." International University of Sheffield on behalf of the International Sports Engineering Association. 2002.

"The Green Report: Engineering Education for a Changing World." American Society for Engineering Education, 1998.

Landis, Raymond B. *Studying Engineering: A Roadmap to a Rewarding Career.* Burbank, CA: Discovery Press, 1995.

LeBold, William K. and Dona J. LeBold. "Women Engineers: A Historical Perspective." Washington, DC: American Society for Engineering Education, 1998.

Love, Sydney F. *Planning and Creating Successful Engineered Designs: Managing the Design Process.* Los Angeles: Advanced Professional Development Incorporated, 1986.

National Science Foundation. "Women, Minorities and Persons with Disabilities in Science and Engineering: 2000." Washington, DC: Sept. 2000.

Peters, Robert L. *Getting What You Came For: The Smart Student's Guide to Earning a Master's or Ph.D.* New York: Farrar, Straus and Giroux, 1997.

Peterson, George D. "Engineering Criteria 2000: A Bold New Change Agent." Washington, DC: American Society for Engineering Education, 1998.

Petroski, Henry. *Invention by Design: How Engineers Get from Thought to Thing.* Cambridge: Harvard University Press, 1996.

———. *To Engineer is Human: The Role of Failure in Successful Design.* New York: Vintage Books, 1992.

———. *The Evolution of Useful Things: How Everyday Artifacts—From Forks and Pins to Paper Clips and Zippers—Came to be as They Are.* New York: Vintage Books, 1992.

Subic, A.J., and S.J. Haake. *The Engineering of Sport: Research, Development and Innovation.* Oxford: Blackwell Science, 2000.

Tieger, Paul and Barbara Barron-Tieger. *Do What You Are: Discover the Perfect Career for You through the Secrets of Personality Type.* Boston: Little, Brown and Company, 1995.

Tietsen, Jill S. and Kristy A Schloss with Carter, Bishop, and Kravits. *Keys to Engineering Success.* New Jersey: Prentice Hall, 2001.

"Women, Minorities, and Persons with Disabilities in Science and Engineering: 1996." Washington, DC: The National Science Foundation, 1996.

Zolli, Andrew. *Catalog of Tomorrow: Trends Shaping Your Future.* Indianapolis: Que and Tech TV, 2002.

About the Author

Celeste Baine is a biomedical engineer and director of the Engineering Education Service Center, a company dedicated to the advancement of engineering education. She is also editor of "The Pre-Engineering Times" monthly newsletter and author of *Is There an Engineer Inside You: A Comprehensive Guide to Career Decisions in Engineering* and *The Fantastical Engineer: A Thrillseeker's Guide to Careers in Theme Park Engineering.*

About the National Society of Professional Engineers

The National Society of Professional Engineers (NSPE) is the only engineering society that represents individual engineering professionals and licensed engineers (PEs) across all disciplines. Founded in 1934, NSPE strengthens the engineering profession by promoting engineering licensure and ethics, enhancing the engineer image, advocating and protecting PEs' legal rights at the national and state levels, publishing news of the profession, providing continuing education opportunities, and much more. NSPE serves some 50,000 members and the public through 53 state and territorial societies and more than 500 chapters.

National Society of Professional Engineers®

Index

2-piccc ball, 85
3-piece ball, 85
active control systems, 43
Adelson, Jeremy, 59
Adidas, 29, 55, 70
aerodynamics, 28–29, 33–34, 48–49, 51
Aeronautics Internet Textbook, 33, 35
alloy, 84
aluminum, 52
American Bowling Congress, 23, 25
American Society of Testing Materials, 43
anatomy, 15, 42
angler, 84
archery, 58
arena, 81–82
AstroTurf, 80
AutoCAD, 52–53
balata balls, 27, 84
bamboo, 40
Barch, Dan, 10, 69
baseball, 16, 42–45, 48, 64, 72, 79, 84–85
basketball, 15–16, 36, 58, 68–69
bat, 15, 42–44
bats, 15, 42–43, 45, 48, 85
bearings, 37, 84

bicycle, 11, 15, 18, 51–52, 59, 64, 68
biology, 15, 76
biomechanics, 15, 42, 67, 68
biomedical engineering, 16, 67, 88
blank, 84
bodysuits, 55
boron, 28
bowling, 23–25, 58, 68, 84
Breese, Jeff, 10, 79
Bromley, Kristan, 48
CAD, 21, 24, 39
CAD/CAM, 21
carbon fiber, 40, 52
carve, 84
Chao, Bing-Ling, 10, 29
Chapman, John W., 10, 39
chemical engineering, 16, 27, 51, 55, 76, 79
chemistry, 15, 27, 75–76
civil engineering, 15, 16, 79
classical engineering, 14
coefficient of restitution, 29, 43
Columbia 300, 23–24
communication, 11
Computer Aided Tracking System, 23, 25
concept, 17, 20, 55
cooperative education, (co-op) 11, 84

core, 24–25, 33, 84–85
court floors, 15
courts, 16, 33–34
coverstock, 84
creative engineering, 9, 14, 17
Crosskate, 36
cutting-edge research, 15
deck, 84
digital audio, 54
digital video special effects, 72
dimples, 28, 84
drag, 28, 33, 37, 49, 55, 58–59, 65
drivers, 28–30, 65
DuPont, 18, 27
durometer, 84
E5, 52
Easton, 42, 53
Edison, Thomas, 11
electrical engineering, 15–16, 25, 40,
    47, 54, 67, 71, 79
entertainment, 14, 42, 45, 71–72, 74
Entrepreneurship Competition, 36
equipment, 11, 14–15, 17–18, 20, 23,
    27–28, 30, 36–37, 39–40, 43, 45,
    47–48, 54, 56, 58–60, 63– 64, 73
Exploratorium, 21, 50, 86
extreme sports, 11, 48
fakie, 84
Farabaugh, Rebecca A.,10, 27
fast action rod, 84
Fédération Internationale de Bobsleigh
et de Tobaganning, 48, 50
felt, 20, 27, 33, 46, 54–55
FieldTurf, 80
fish finder, 40–41
fishing, 39–41, 48, 58, 84–85
fishing poles, 40, 48

fishing rod, 39
foot placement, 14, 67
football, 16, 44, 58, 63–64, 68, 72–73, 80
Fox Sports, 71, 73
Freebord Manufacturing, 10, 20
friction, 23–24, 33, 37, 47, 49
Glass, Stacie, 10, 46
G-Max rating, 79, 80, 84
golf, 11, 14, 27–29, 30, 48, 84–85
GPS, 30, 40–41
granular infill synthetic, 79
graphite, 28, 30, 40, 43, 84
grind, 16, 84
Hanen, Laurant, 18
Hawk, Tony, 20, 22
health, 14, 63
heavy test line, 84
helmets, 11, 16, 43, 53, 63, 64–65
hockey, 36–38, 59, 63–64
HOK Sports Facilities Group, 80
Humphries, Jay F., 10, 57
Hutter, Chris, 10, 71
hydraulics, 79
industrial, 16, 69, 71
inertia, 23, 29, 65
injuries, 15–16, 32, 34, 43, 59,
    64–65, 68–69, 79–80
Injury Surveillance System, 43
Intellifibers, 47
International Tennis Federation, 33–35
Iron Byron, 28, 85
juiced, 85
K2, 38, 46–47, 49, 51, 53
kayak, 55
Kellogg's, 75
Kentucky derby, 72
Lieu, Dennis K., 10, 63

Loeffler, Don, 32
McNamee, Mark, 10, 42
manufacturing, 16–17, 24, 28–29, 34,
    41, 44–45, 49, 60, 65, 69, 77, 79
martial arts, 63–64
materials, 11, 14–18, 21, 28–29, 32,
    34, 38–45, 47–49, 51–53, 56, 60,
    65–66, 69, 79, 82
materials engineers, 11, 28, 69
math, 14, 17, 27, 39, 46, 54, 72,
    75–77, 79–80
mechanical engineering, 11, 15–17,
    20, 23, 28, 36, 39–40, 42, 46–47,
    56–57, 63–64, 67, 69, 76, 79, 85
mechanics, 14, 63
Milliken, Kyle, 10, 17
models, 20, 55, 64
mountain biking, 36, 51
movement, 14–15, 65, 69, 73
NASCAR, 65
National Society of Professional
Engineers, 10, 88
Nike, 16, 68–70
O'Neal, Shaquille, 20
Ocif, Jennifer, 10, 11, 67
Ollie, 21, 85
Olympics, 15, 23, 46, 48–49, 54–56,
    59, 63, 67, 68, 81, 82
Page, James, 10, 36
Paralympic games, 59
parathletes, 58
patents, 11, 20, 39
Penn, 33–34, 41
Peon, Roberto, 72
physical fitness, 14
physics, 15, 24, 33, 42, 46, 48, 49,
    63, 72, 86

piezoelectric device, 85
Ping Pong, 58
Piumarta, Tim, 21
plastic, 16, 18, 28, 40, 65, 67, 85
polymer, 18, 27
Pre-Olympic Congress, 15
Pro/ENGINEER, 52–53
problem solving, 15
prototype, 20, 24–25, 36, 39, 44,
    46–47, 49, 60, 65, 67, 68–69
Pure Fishing, 10, 39, 41
racquet, 32–34
radius of gyration, 85
Rawlings Sporting Goods, 43
reduce pollution, 14
Reebok, 11, 67–68, 70
reel seat, 85
resin, 18, 27, 84
Reuse-A-Shoe, 16
Santa Cruz Skateboards, 21
science, 14–15, 34, 46, 54, 67, 75–77
scoreboards, 11
sealed bearing, 85
sensors, 25, 47, 51, 69
simple machine, 51
skate parks, 21
skateboarding, 11, 20–21, 64, 68
skeleton, 46, 48, 50
ski, 14–15, 18, 36, 46–47, 54, 60,
    63, 72
skiing, 11, 36, 47, 49, 54, 58, 64
slow action rod, 85
snowboard, 20, 46–47
snowboarding, 20, 46, 47, 49, 64
soccer, 16, 68–69
software engineers, 11, 40
Soule, Chris, 48

Special Olympics, 59
speed skating, 37, 46, 68, 72
Speranza, Dan, 10, 23
sports science, 14–15
Sportvision, Inc, 72
SprinTurf, 80
stadiums, 11, 45, 80, 82
Stanford University, 20
stiffness, 21, 29, 40, 47
sting, 15, 42–43
Strand, Steen, 10, 20
street surf, 20
stride length, 14
Surlyn® 27–28, 84–85
sweet spot, 29, 34, 42–43, 85
swimming, 11, 54, 55–56
swing speed, 14, 27
Taylormade-Adidas Golf Co, 29
technology, 11, 14–16, 23, 27, 30, 39,
    42–44, 47, 48, 54, 56, 60, 71–72, 82
tennis, 16, 32–34, 58, 68
Terry, Georgena, 10, 51
Terry Bicycles, 51, 53
timing systems, 15, 49
titanium, 28, 33, 43, 52, 59, 84
Toronto Skydome, 79
Townsend, Robert, 17
Track, 23, 25, 82
Truck, 85
U.S. Olympic Committee, 54
United States Golf Association, 28
Utah Olympic Park, 15
ventilation, 64
vibration, 29, 39, 43, 47–48, 51
voice synthesis, 54
volleyball, 58–59, 68
Wall Street, 20

water skis, 48
weight room, 16
Westenburg, Tom, 10, 54
wheel, 85
wheelchairs, 58, 59
Willis, Betsy F., 10, 75–76
Wilson Sporting Goods, 30, 32, 44–45
Wimbledon, 33
wind tunnel, 33, 44, 60, 65
Woodruff, Sophie, 17
woods, 28, 30
Woods, Tiger, 14, 27
yellow first-down line, 72

Other Books by Celeste Baine

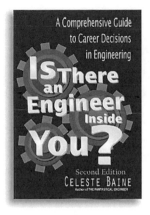

Is There an Engineer Inside You?

Turn yourself into a top-notch engineering student and become a successful engineer with the ideas and information in this one-of-a-kind resource. Get yourself on the path to a challenging, rewarding, and prosperous career as an engineer by getting inside each discipline, learning the differences and making educated choices. Updated and now covering 27 different branches of engineering, *Is There an Engineer Inside You* is packed with suggestions and has tremendous advice on thriving in an engineering student environment.

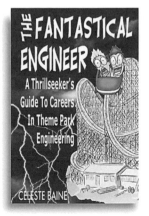

The Fantastical Engineer

This title describes how engineers make the magic that is every theme park, amusement park, roller coaster, aquarium, zoo, cinema, sporting event, or trade show. Book features articles from industry experts and tells how to survive in this fast-paced and changeable industry. You can also preview the future of themed attraction design in this one-of-a-kind career guide.

NOTES:

NOTES: